BASICS
FASHION MANAGEMENT

FASHION RETAILING

From Managing to Merchandising

Dimitri Koumbis

Bloomsbury Visual Arts

An imprint of Bloomsbury Publishing Plc

50 Bedford Square	1385 Broadway
London	New York
WC1B 3DP	NY 10018
UK	USA

www.bloomsbury.com

Bloomsbury is a registered trademark of Bloomsbury Publishing Plc

British Library Cataloguing-in-Publication Data

A catalog record for this book is available from the British Library.

ISBN: PB:978-2-9404-9623-5
ePDF: 978-1-4725-6862-5

Library of Congress Cataloging-in-Publication Data

Koumbis, Dimitri.
Fashion retailing : from managing to merchandising / Dimitri Koumbis.
pages   cm
Includes bibliographical references and index.
ISBN 978-2-940496-23-5 (alk. paper)
1. Fashion merchandising. 2. Retail trade. I. Title.
HD9940.A2K68 2014
746.9'20688--dc23   2013036269

Cover image: Marni flagship store, Las Vegas (photographer: Donato Sardella),
copyright: Sybarite Architects

Design: Pony Ltd.

www.ponybox.co.uk

Printed and bound in China

1 MEMORABLE STORE DESIGN

H&M, one of retail's leading mid-market
fast fashion retailers, draws its consumers
in with beautifully designed exteriors that
seamlessly blend into the vernacular.
Pictured is its Miami store, where the
white stucco facade and neon lights pay
homage to the Art Deco city it is part of.

TABLE OF CONTENTS

INTRODUCTION

Every day, consumers visit retailers both online and at their physical store locations, looking for those items that will satisfy a need based on emotion or necessity. They look to their favorite brands to help them feel confident and beautiful, or simply to provide them with warmth for the season. The retailers consumers turn to are more than physical spaces for products; they are well-oiled machines that strategically plan years in advance for what customers are purchasing today. Retailing is an industry already embedded within the landscape of our built environment, and as it continues to expand throughout cyberspace, retailers are anxious to extend their brands to the farthest communities across the globe.

Fashion Retailing aims to provide its readers with a basic understanding of how contemporary retailers operate, primarily within a brick and mortar setting. A brief introduction is given on the history of retail before moving into retailer types and the differences between on-site and off-site retailing. A broad look at consumer behavior, and markets and how the markets differ within emerging international retail communities starts a deeper conversation about retailers as a whole—from corporate offices to the shop floor.

This book is divided into six sections that will take readers on a journey from the history of retail to e-commerce in a digital age. Various topics are discussed, such as employee management, loss prevention, and visual merchandising as it pertains to the store level and is facilitated through retailers' corporate offices. Each section is followed with an interview and a case study that reiterate the chapter's message, offering deeper insight to various jobs and successful international brands.

The exciting, fast-paced world of retail keeps all stakeholders—consumers and retailers—working together to provide a lucrative industry that marries fashion, design, and commerce and gives consumers a plethora of aesthetically pleasing and business-savvy brands to choose from.

1 THROUGH THE LOOKING GLASS
Window displays allow retailers to tell fictitious stories about the fashion brands they sell in their stores.

Introduction

Chapter 1

In chapter 1, the difference between the retailer and retailing is explored, looking at those attributes that make brands successful. We then move into the various retail types and look at what differentiates one store type from another. On-site and off-site retailing is touched on, followed by a discussion of various multichannel approaches that allow retailers to create a solid brand in a competitive marketplace.

Chapter 2

Understanding how consumers think is incredibly important for retailers, as it allows them to make decisions within their establishments that will keep shoppers coming back season after season.

This chapter explores various consumer behavior models and looks at consumer markets on national and international levels. Having a solid understanding of the market in which a store is located allows corporate managers to make more informed decisions when they make seasonal product purchases or create marketing plans and allows store teams to properly merchandise the product once it has been received.

Chapter 3

Chapter 3 begins to unveil the inner workings of retailers, providing the audience with a greater understanding of the role they play in the supply channel. After discussing various corporate-level positions, the chapter moves into the strategic planning process and how it supports store-level teams.

To finish the chapter, corporate social responsibility (CSR) is defined and the reason it is important for retailers to build solid CSR plans into their business models is discussed.

Chapter 4

Chapter 4 deals with store management and provides valuable insight into how stores operate regarding managerial roles and the decisions managers make when hiring, training, and developing store associates. Moving into store logistics processes, readers will learn about how product is moved from distribution centers to stores, facilitated by those roles under corporate merchandisers, such as planners and allocators. The chapter concludes with talking in detail about the loss prevention tactics utilized to avoid high shrink rates caused by internal and external theft.

Chapter 5

One of the most coveted positions at the store level is the visual merchandiser, which is introduced in chapter 5. In this chapter, readers learn the difference between merchandising and visual merchandising, as well as the importance of visual merchandising in the store environment, taking into account customer accessibility and corporate seasonal floor-set direction. This chapter informs readers about how visual aesthetics can positively affect store sales, especially when the merchandising team utilizes company sales reports to create displays and make product moves based on business need.

Chapter 6

The final chapter in the book looks at trending areas in the retail sector. E-tailing is discussed in more detail to give readers a better understanding of how young the e-commerce industry is and the potential it provides for retailers to expand their brands into a more global presence. The chapter also explores the methods by which e-commerce-only retailers expand into the brick and mortar world through the utilization of various marketing strategies. Chapter 6 concludes with a look at technology and what consumers may hope to see next from retailers in the store environment.

Fashion Retailing is an introductory text that provides readers with an opportunity to better understand how retailers operate and offers a starting point to further develop their careers in the retail sector. It is a text that combines strong imagery with informative case studies and interviews, as well as concept skill-building exercises, to help readers understand just how exciting this industry is to work in.

"My first job was in retail at the age of 14, and I have worked in the industry ever since."

Rachel Roy, fashion designer

1

WHAT IS RETAILING?

1 THE SKY IS THE LIMIT

Shoppers have a plethora of shops to choose from within the Pavilion shopping mall, Bukit Bintang, Kuala Lumpur, Malaysia. Large shopping areas like this allow multiple retailers to be housed under one roof, making it easier to shop during seasonal weather.

Retailing is a lucrative trade that spans the globe, accounting for much of the international job market in terms of employment and income. For many, the retail industry provides a means of income not only for its stakeholders but also for the communities in which it thrives (think about the tax revenue generated!). Retailers are quick to adapt to consumer needs, ensuring the latest trends are at their disposal. Advances in technology have allowed for a more seamless relationship between consumers and retailers, literally putting retailers and their goods at consumers' fingertips. From the historic method of bartering goods to contemporary approaches in e-commerce, retail is a rapidly expanding industry that provides consumers with virtually unlimited options for the fashion-forward products they wish to indulge in.

The history of retail

Retail is a relatively young industry that is continually adapting to meet the changes in culture and technology but, even more so, to satisfy consumer demands. The concept of shopping in a physical store for a specific type or genre of goods developed rapidly as nations became more industrialized and mass-produced goods became more readily available.

To better understand contemporary retail environments, it is important to first understand their origin. The retail landscape today is a metropolis compared to the original trading posts that were erected in early civilizations. These trading posts were a means for providing colonies with basic necessities, such as food, clothing, and shelter. During this time, settlers relied on a bartering system, or trading one product for another, whether it be agricultural goods supplied by local farmers or pelts and meats supplied by trappers. This was a simple system, whereby goods acted as the monetary unit for purchasing other goods.

Toward the end of the nineteenth century, these trading posts began to compartmentalize like goods to make shopping easier for customers and were referred to as *general stores*. Eventually, general stores gave way to limited stores, or stores that carried a single classification of goods, such as apparel, shoes, and accessories. Today, we refer to limited stores as specialty stores, which are discussed in greater detail later in this chapter.

As technology began to evolve, especially after the Industrial Revolution, shopping became a leisurely pastime whereby people could see the newest items that these technological advances were able to produce. This also allowed a greater number of finished goods to be sold, which led to competitive pricing and a greater variety of options for consumers. As demand for these products grew, the introduction of the department store became a blessing, allowing patrons to browse and buy a wide variety of goods and services under one roof. Some of the earliest known department stores are David Jones, Australia; Marshall Field & Company, US; and Le Bon Marché, France, all opening up their doors in the mid- to late 1800s.

2

2-3 HISTORIC RETAIL

Retailing has continually evolved, from the early days of Native American trade in the US colonies to the erection of specialty and department stores, which began to introduce customer service initiatives to draw in patrons. The scenes depicted here show the early years of the retail industry, capturing the beginning of a global industry.

3

"When this business was founded, it sought to win public confidence through service, for it was my conviction then, as it is now, that nothing else than right service to the public results in mutual understanding and satisfaction between customer and merchant. It was for this reason that our business was founded upon the eternal principle of the Golden Rule."

James Cash Penney, on his first general stores, Golden Rule Store, c. 1900s

Understanding the difference between retailing and the retailer

It is a common assumption that retailers sell a specific product type, but it is important to know that a retailer is a business that sells both goods and services to the consumer for personal use. While products such as fashion apparel and accessories, home hard and soft goods, and electronics are often what we identify as that which the vast majority of retailers provide, it helps to acknowledge the other products and services offered, to better understand the term.

For instance, dentists sell their services, providing patients with dental exams, cleanings, and X-rays. These are not tangible items you put in a bag and take home, per se, but are a retail service provided for personal need. After a stressful school term, you are excited to utilize a gift card for a massage that your family gave you. You see the massage therapist and trade your gift card for an hour-long massage. While you don't physically walk away from the session with a tangible good, you did pay for a service that helps to alleviate stress and tension. The service product in this case was the massage, and the monetary payment was the gift card. Looking at various services outside of fashion retail helps to better understand the definition of retailer and will allow you to recognize such goods and services in the future.

4

5

After identifying retailers, it is important to differentiate between who they are and the strategies they employ, hoping to draw in new customers while engaging and retaining the current ones. Retailing is the various business strategies and activities that add value to the goods and services sold to consumers for their personal use. A retailer may introduce new props and/or fixtures on the sales floor or create an in-store marketing campaign in an effort to promote sales. Both of these tactics can be described as retailing activities or strategies that will add value to the products or services offered to consumers.

RETAILING ACTIVITIES

A retailer will use various retailing activities in an effort to support both the consumer and employer. The following activities can be used alone or in various combinations to accomplish a specific goal that the retailer may have:

× Visual merchandising and display.
× Advertising or marketing.
× Customer service and interaction.
× Branding.
× Store design.
× Logistics.

4-5   HAVING THE RIGHT MIX OF RETAILING ACTIVITIES

Retailers will seek to find a good combination of various retailing activities to help promote the brand while drawing in and keeping consumers. Harrods uses store design and visual merchandising as an aesthetic to interest customers. A recent collaboration between Natalia Vodianova, Dior, and Harrods is a marketing tactic that draws customers' interest while informing them of new products.

Understanding the difference between retailing and the retailer

Supply channels

When discussing the retailer, one must understand its role in the consumer marketplace. The retailer acts as the link between manufacturers and consumers in the retail supply chain. A supply chain is the set of firms that produce and distribute goods and services to consumers. Think of it as a linear formation that starts with production and ends with consumption. In between production and consumption are subsystems that help with the flow of goods. These subsystems are the retailer and the wholesaler.

A wholesaler is a firm within the supply chain that:

× Purchases goods from manufacturers and/or other wholesalers.
× Takes title of the purchased goods.
× Stores, handles, and distributes these goods.
× Resells goods at a later time to retailers (or directly to consumers).

While the wholesaler performs many of the same tasks the retailer does, it typically provides goods directly to only the retailer, whereas the retailer provides goods directly to only the end user. However, with the Internet becoming a major source for product procurement, wholesalers are beginning to form relationships directly with consumers, bypassing retail sales channels altogether. This situation can be seen in companies such as Costco Wholesale, an American-based wholesale company that sells various products and services both on-site and off-site. Consumers can order directly from the wholesaler, whereby buying in bulk can provide them with a generous discount per unit.

FLOW OF GOODS

MANUFACTURERS

Convert raw goods to fibers, spin and dye yarns, and either sell to wholesalers or work directly with retailers on in-house-designed goods.

WHOLESALERS

Take title of and store large quantities of the goods produced by manufacturers and supply these goods predominately to retailers, but often directly to consumers too.

Service integration

The concept of firms providing multiple activities and services throughout the retail supply chain is known as vertical service integration. There are three types of vertical service integration that occur in the retail sector. The first, forward integration, is when a manufacturer provides one or more sets of activities in the retail supply chain, therefore retaining control of its distributors. Ralph Lauren not only has control of design and manufacturing for its product, but also provides wholesale stock to many department stores and private boutiques both in the US and overseas. You can also find Ralph Lauren product in several private label retail outlets, as well as online.

Backward integration is when a firm performs limited manufacturing and wholesaling activities or has limited control of its suppliers. An example of a firm that employs backward integration is IKEA, which heavily stocks its product in a warehouse that also acts as the retail venue. IKEA is able to house much of its product, alleviating the need for off-site warehouse locations and distribution centers. In this case, they are acting as both the wholesaler and retailer.

Lastly, balanced integration is when a firm manufactures, wholesales, and retails its products, having complete control from production to distribution. American Apparel is an example of balanced integration, as it is a firm that designs, manufactures, and sells its products in-house and also offers wholesale products and private label production. Balanced integration allows them to make conscious business decisions that have the potential to affect a greater scope of the company.

6 FASHION SUPPLY CHAINS

Each member of the supply chain plays an integral role in fashion retailing. Simultaneously, as the flow of goods moves from manufacturers to consumers, the flow of information regarding use of goods and services moves from consumers back to manufacturers.

RETAILERS

Sell goods directly to consumers for personal use. They take into account consumer needs and preferences when purchasing products from wholesalers and manufacturers.

CONSUMERS

Purchase goods based on various motives and turn either to retailers or directly to wholesalers to meet those personal needs.

FLOW OF INFORMATION   6

Classification of retailers

With a better understanding of the difference between a retailer and the strategies employed to promote the sale of its goods, it is time to define the different types of retailers. Retailer typology refers to the classification of a retailer's selling space, whether it is on-site or off-site, and helps consumers further differentiate a retailer's goods.

Retailers' on-site selling spaces are referred to as *brick and mortar*, a term derived from early construction methods and used to imply the physical space, or location, that a retailer utilizes for selling its goods and services. We use the term *brick and mortar* to refer to only those physical spaces that consumers can shop from. Internet-based businesses are not brick and mortar plants because you cannot physically visit their locations. However, many retailers will supplement their brick and mortar locations with e-tailing (discussed later in this chapter) strategies, such as the Internet or catalogs and direct mail. Following are the most common retailer types identified when discussing brick and mortar locations for the on-site approach: boutiques, specialty shops, department stores, off-price merchants, fashion manufacturer's outlets, discount operations, and warehouse clubs.

Boutiques

A boutique is a retailer that sells product to a niche market, usually high-end, where there is a limited quantity of goods sold at higher prices. The word boutique has a French origin, meaning "shop" and was a term used to denote those early establishments that sold one-line specialty goods to consumers, such as fabric and jewelry. Today, the word *boutique* usually refers to retailers that have a single or small quantity of brick and mortar locations and sell a combination of goods not typically found at mass-market retailers. Boutiques will often have small selling square footages and will keep most products on the sales floor due to the limited quantities and lack of back-stock space.

Specialty shops

Specialty shops are those retail stores that typically sell a specific product classification and related accessories. They may cater to a specific demographic or product assortment, but usually the range of merchandise is very limited. In specialty stores, the size of the selling square footage may vary, but at each location, the concept of the retail shop always remains the same.

The success of specialty shops is contingent upon three things:

× A broad assortment of the merchandise sold (e.g., one style of shirt in a large number of colors).
× The size of the brick and mortar location must accommodate easy visibility of all goods, allowing consumers to enter and exit quickly.
× Excellent customer service must be provided.

As a specialty shop begins to multiply in the number of locations, the cost of business-related expenses is reduced. The buying department may get bigger discounts for buying larger quantities of product, or insurance premiums for employees may drop due to a larger investment in the insurance policy. These decreases in business expenses may allow the specialty shop to invest in subspecialty shops, or spin-offs, of the original shop that cater to consumers who are looking for a more defined product assortment based on its original offerings.

For example, Gap opened two subspecialty shops to cater to those consumers who trusted the company name but were looking for a specific item not often carried in Gap stores across the globe. The first, GapKids, sells fashion apparel and accessories to parents with infants and young children. This product assortment resembles the fashions you would find at Gap, but sizes cater to the children's retail sector. Later, Gap opened GapBody, which offers a large assortment of intimates and accessories for both men and women, including bath toiletries and accessories. These subspecialty shops are often located near their parent company, which entices the consumer to shop at both specialty and subspecialty shops.

Department stores

Those retailers that offer a wide range of merchandise comprising both hard and soft goods are referred to as department stores. The term *department store* is taken from historic stores that used to compartmentalize their goods for consumers, making it easier to navigate through, as well as offering one-stop shopping. They have large selling square footages, typically comprising multiple floors. If a department store carries a full product assortment of both hard and soft goods, it is referred to as a full-line department store. Harrods and Macy's are considered full-line department stores due to their wide variety of both fashion apparel and home goods.

A specialized department store is one that offers a large mix of fashion apparel and accessories only. This type of department store is becoming more prominent in our retail landscape due to the introduction and success of the discount retailer (see discount operations, p. 23). Department stores will often have a flagship location in major cities. This is their biggest store with the largest assortment of goods and services. To cater to smaller demographics, they will open branches or spin-off stores in suburban areas. This allows them to use the highly recognized retail identity but scale back on size and product assortment for smaller locations and/or more challenging markets.

Classification of retailers

8

9

7-9 RETAIL TYPOLOGY

Understanding the various retail types helps to understand the overall goal of the retailer, giving a better understanding of how its corporate offices may work in terms of buying, marketing, and visual merchandising.

Classification of retailers

Off-price merchants

As many consumers became more cost aware of the fast fashions they were purchasing, retailers began to capitalize on the growing trend of discounted shops that offered last-season or overstock goods. One of the pioneering leaders in this trend was Frieda Loehmann, who in 1921 began purchasing overstock and last season's goods to sell them to women at discounted prices.

Off-price merchants are those retailers that offer a mix of hard and soft goods to consumers at significantly lower price points than are found at traditional retailers. They will purchase goods that have become out of season (or dates), at discounted rates, from traditional retailers and will then sell them to consumers for a percentage off the manufacturer's suggested retail price, or MSRP, for short.

Resident buying offices will work with vendors to procure overpurchased quantities of goods or items no longer selling in stores, in an effort to buy them at a fraction of the wholesale cost and then resell them. This type of buying behavior is known as opportunistic purchasing, whereby resident buying offices that source these goods are unable to reorder items that sell out in their stores. Due to the product assortment that is obtained through opportunistic purchasing, off-price merchants will situate themselves at a comfortable distance from traditional retailers so that their prices and products do not compete.

Unlike traditional retailers, off-price merchants often lack the quality and customer service found at specialty shops and department stores. Their main objective is to pass savings on to consumers while still making a profit. Often, their stores are less aesthetically pleasing, lack a cohesive concept, and don't rely on merchandising strategies to sell the product. They cultivate the mentality, what you see is what you get (WYSIWYG) and once it's gone, it's gone. This is great motivation for the shopper who purchases only discounted goods, refusing to pay the MSRP for an item.

Following the idea of off-price merchants, three other retail types emerged: fashion manufacturer's outlets, discount operations, and warehouse clubs. All three act in the same capacity as the off-price merchant but provide different selling environments for the consumer.

Fashion manufacturer's outlets

Retail establishments that sell a single brand's product assortment at discounted prices off the MSRP are interchangeably called fashion manufacturer's outlets or factory stores. This is a fast-growing retailer type because it allows retailers to provide a significant discount for their out-of-season, damaged, or overassorted goods while still maintaining the brand image seen in their traditional store locations. Fashion manufacturer's outlets are typically grouped together, renting their spaces from major leasing companies who own the land and the facilities (much like suburban malls).

Major property-leasing agents include Tanger Outlets and Premium Outlets based in the United States and McArthurGlenn Designer Outlet based in Europe. The stores within these outlet malls range from midmarket to high-end retailers, such as Gap, Levi's, DKNY, Prada, and Gucci. Typically, these outlet malls are located in suburban areas, far from the full-price competition, where destination locations can be created for consumers and brand loyalists.

Discount operations

Discount operations or value-oriented retailers are those that offer a diversified assortment of hard and soft goods at significantly lower prices. These retailers carry well-known brand names but offer them at lower prices due to the large number of stock they are able to purchase, passing these discounts on to the consumer. Often, these discount operations are referred to as big-box retailers because of their large selling square footage and lack of architectural interest.

Big-box retailers strive to keep operating costs low, while producing large quantities of their stock. In the past, these retailers have been anchor stores in strip malls (shopping centers) but recently have moved to become more of a destination location, in a similar way to the factory outlet malls. Examples of these types of retailers are Walmart, with headquarters in the United States, and Tesco, based in the UK. Both are very successful, but Walmart has led the race for years in both profits and number of stores worldwide, as it continues to quickly expand in Asian and South American markets.

Warehouse clubs

Lastly are the wholesalers of the retail types: warehouse clubs. Warehouse clubs purchase and house large quantities of assorted hard and soft goods and sell these items in bulk to consumers, at discounted rates. The discount comes from buying multiple units of the same product as well as charging a membership fee that is often required to be a member of these clubs. Because these retailers move through merchandise in such large quantities, they are able to keep markup to a minimal, passing the savings on to their club members.

On-site vs. off-site retailing

As discussed previously, on-site approaches to retailing typically involve the brick and mortar location where a consumer will shop. Aside from this traditional method, there are quickly emerging trends, such as pop-up shops and mobile retailers being used to introduce new brands to the marketplace. These channels are less expensive than their brick and mortar cousins and allow retailers to test markets before securing permanent physical space.

Off-site retailing

Off-site retailing is the fast-growing method for fashion retail sales due mostly from the increase in Internet use across the globe, whether it be through personal computers or smartphone applications. Electronic retailing, or e-tailing, as it is commonly referred to, is when a retailer uses the Internet to provide retailing transactions, such as browsing, purchasing, or returning, to consumers.

E-tailing has long begun to rival traditional on-site retailing because of the convenience and global accessibility to consumers. Consumers are researching goods prior to purchasing, looking at multiple sites for the best price and consumer reviews on both the product and the company. Many will quickly secure their online order when satisfied with their product choice, especially with free shipping options becoming more frequent. When a retailer offers both on-site and e-tailing purchasing channels, this is referred to as *brick and click*, a term derived from the "brick" of brick and mortar and the click sound that a mouse makes as you navigate through web pages of product. There are two other off-site methods to be aware of, though they are not as popular when used alone: catalogs and televending.

ON-SITE RETAILING
× Provides consumers with a total brand experience.
× Allows consumers to try on product prior to purchasing, thus alleviating returns.
× Often provides deeper discounts on sales in order to move product out of the brick and mortar location in anticipation of new arrivals.
× Provides employment within communities.
× Can easily offer online shopping within the store location.
× Is more expensive to operate.

OFF-SITE RETAILING
× Provides the ease of shopping without consumer traffic during weekends, holidays, etc.
× Often offers free shipping and return.
× New trends in fashion are often showcased prior to hitting brick and mortar stores.
× Overhead costs are much less expensive.
× Consumers have no sense of connection to the brand.

Catalogs

Catalogs are the printed materials that are sent via traditional mail delivery systems, which are also referred to as direct marketing. A well-known US catalog retailer, Spiegel, sent its first direct marketing piece in the early 1900s, offering women's fashion apparel and home furnishings. This was a successful channel for the retailer until the advent of the Internet made the catalog an obsolete channel for attracting consumer sales. This, combined with many changing hands of ownership, has caused the retailer to become unrecognizable, though a website is currently in place today. More successful catalog companies like Red Envelope and Fingerhut (both US-based e-tailers) will offer in-house credit options for easier purchasing capabilities. However, they are still supplementing their direct mail marketing with Internet sites.

Televending

Televending, or video shopping, is when consumers purchase goods through cable network television shows. The most widely known, QVC, has been a successful televending channel since 1986, when it first began in eastern Pennsylvania. The acronym stands for quality, value, and convenience, which is reiterated by the many products that have celebrity endorsements and over 200 million viewers in the US, UK, Japan, Germany, and Italy.

Many infomercials seen on late-night television that aim to capture a specific demographic are also considered televending. The market for this type of product is very expansive, and many entrepreneurs have become overnight successes for selling their products through this channel.

Today, it is important to utilize both on-site and off-site methods, allowing the greatest number of consumers to be reached in the shortest amount of time. This is an approach known as multichannel retailing, which will be discussed in the next section.

"If there's one reason we have done better than our peers in the Internet space over the last six years, it is because we have focused like a laser on customer experience, and that really does matter, I think, in any business. It certainly matters online, where word of mouth is so very, very powerful."

Jeff Bezos, CEO of Amazon, 2008

Multichannel retail approaches

When a retailer offers its goods and services through various distribution channels—brick and mortar stores, websites, smartphone applications, or catalogs, it is called multichannel retailing. This allows the retailer to distribute its goods and services to the greatest amount of consumers (or potential consumers) by offering retailing channels that best resonate with them.

Providing consumers with various channels for procuring merchandise may not only increase sales revenue but can also act as a marketing tactic for introducing brands to potential customers, especially in locations where that retailer may not be available.

Multichannel retailing has sparked new trends in the way retailers offer their goods and services, not only because of strong competition, but also because of consumer demand and advances in technology. Some of the trends that have materialized due to a need for change in the way retailers conduct their business are:

× Pop-up shops.
× Spin-offs.
× Exclusive commitments and collaborations.
× Expansions through acquisitions.
× Smartphone applications.
× Lookbooks and catalogs.

It is rare nowadays that a retailer will utilize only one retailing approach, which can severely limit its product offerings or minimize its customer base. Retailers are quickly reaching out to all age groups, offering them the fastest, most convenient method that works best for their lifestyle. As previously discussed, with on-site vs. off-site retailing, it is truly a combination of the two that makes a successful retailer.

OMNI-CHANNEL RETAILING

This is a fairly new term being used in the industry, referring to a seamlessly integrated approach to the customer experience, linking what was once multichannel approaches (brick and mortar, online, apps, etc.) into one experience whereby the consumer can easily navigate between each channel.

What this is ultimately allowing is for retailers to refrain from differentiating between online sales, store sales, etc., and for looking at the process as one sale. While e-sales continue to grow there may come a time when multichannel retailing is replaced with omni-channel retailing.

WEBSITES

SMART MOBILES

GAMING CONSOLES

ONLINE CATALOG

CONSUMER

PHYSICAL STORE

SOCIAL MEDIA

COMPUTERS

KIOSKS

10

10 MULTICHANNEL APPROACHES

Just as the consumer is using multichannel approaches to reach their favorite retailers, retailers are employing the same tools to reach out to consumers. The need for tech-savvy individuals who also understand demographics is vital to contemporary retailers' success.

Interview: Kyle Muller — Shop owner

RÉSUMÉ HIGHLIGHTS

2001–2004
Studied Fine Arts, Studio Art (Painting and Photography) at The University of Texas at Austin.

2004–2007
Worked as a graphic designer for local newspaper and small design firms in Austin, Texas, designing corporate branding and marketing collateral.

2007–2008
Moved to France to work as a professional bicycle tour guide in Paris.

2008–2011
Graphic designer for fashion PR firm, New York City, managing in-house creative services department, designing event/promotional material.

2011–Present
Moved back to Austin, Texas, and launched Sam Hill, a men's clothing store focusing on vintage and private label goods.

"People don't buy what you do . . . they buy why you do it. If you can figure out your 'why' and truly believe in it, others will too."

11 CAREFULLY CURATED

Sam Hill exudes a blended essence of both retail shop and art gallery, providing customers with an array of fashion apparel and accessories, home goods, and gifts.

Interview: Kyle Muller – Shop Owner

Q How did the Sam Hill brand evolve?

A I love clothes and relics from the past and have been obsessed my entire life. I noticed an unfilled niche in Austin for my vision of a highly refined vintage store. I strive to have a standard of inventory that differs from other places in town. I made a conscious decision last year to "really" do it. I had been contemplating the idea for years. I already had a knowledge base for vintage garments and started making connections and now have a few vintage suppliers and a clothing route where I source inventory.

Q What was your first retail job and how did it and future jobs pave the way for your current position?

A I worked a retail job in high school when I was 16. It was a theme restaurant in the mall, and I was a sales associate for the gift shop. I had no interest in the product but enjoyed interacting with people. My most important job in regard to forming my own retail brand was my career as a graphic designer. Branding and marketing were two areas where I gained extensive knowledge, which helped me to create Sam Hill.

Q Can you give us an overview of the daily tasks involved in running a boutique retail shop?

A Currently I have no investors, so I operate with a very limited budget, which means I do everything from finance and accounting to janitorial work and construction. Every day, there are an overwhelming number of tasks that need to be done, but I try to prioritize to start with the most important—what is the one thing I need to do today or what's the one thing that will yield the most rewards.

12-13 HILL COUNTRY AESTHETICS
Sam Hill's contemporary rustic design provides the perfect backdrop for the vintage finds and private label goods sold in the stores.

12

Q Reflecting back on the shop's developmental process, what would you say was the most difficult task to making your vision come to fruition? What was the easiest?

A The most difficult task is finding time and money. Usually when you have one, the other isn't there. You need both to make your vision come to fruition. The easiest task was receiving press and gaining interest from patrons and support from local publications.

Q What advice can you provide to future retail entrepreneurs?

A People don't buy what you do; they buy why you do it. If you can figure out your "why" and truly believe in it, others will too. My vision is to have my own label, creating an international brand with several retail locations.

13

Case study: Harvey Nichols

In the early nineteenth century, an entrepreneur named Benjamin Harvey introduced a linen shop based out of a terraced townhouse in Knightsbridge, London. Upon his passing, Harvey left his namesake to his daughter, who later married a prominent Far East importer, Colonel Nichols. Combining their goods to be sold under one roof, they opened a new shop, appropriately titled Harvey Nichols.

In 1880, a larger space was secured and constructed to showcase the wide variety of linens, oriental rugs, silks, and other luxury goods that Harvey Nichols would sell. After operating for roughly forty years, Harvey Nichols was bought by another prominent retailer, Debenhams, which was later acquired by the Burton Group, based in London, in 1985. Dickson Concepts (International) Ltd out of Hong Kong (which owns other fashion retailers, such as Tod's, Tommy Hilfiger, and American Eagle Outfitters) acquired the stores, later returning them to the private ownership of Dr. Dickson Poon, a prominent businessman who has retail businesses in Europe, Asia, and North America.

"Abstract mannequins with strong poses show consumers the fun side of both the retailer and the designer, making the product and space quickly come alive."

14 THE RIGHT VISUAL MIX

Harvey Nichols seamlessly blends fashion, art, and architecture to create stunning visual displays, both inside and out, that target the contemporary shopper.

14

Harvey Nichols has long since moved from selling linens and oriental rugs and currently provides high-fashion items for men, women, and children. While it has long prided itself on contemporary luxury goods, Harvey Nichols has begun introducing many diffusion lines and has since incorporated a larger percentage of private labels in hopes of keeping costs down and providing savings to its consumers.

This high-brow concept competes with other department stores, such as Barneys and Nordstrom, which also tend to attract a younger, more fashion-forward demographic. The company prides itself on customer service, for which it is well known, offering such services as personal shopping, home delivery, and an amazing "click and collect" service, which allows consumers to shop online and pick up their purchases at brick and mortar locations.

Case study: Harvey Nichols

Contemporary design, inside and out

Besides their large selection of designer goods and flawless customer service, Harvey Nichols provides beautifully designed retail spaces for its consumers to shop in. From its traditional storefronts in London to the more contemporary exteriors seen in new construction across the Middle East, the architecture and interior design seamlessly marries both form and function, creating an environment that beautifully showcases its products and allows fluidity in consumer circulation.

Once inside, architectural detailing, strong lighting, and memorable displays keep shoppers engaged, allowing them to become part of the Harvey Nichols world. Abstract mannequins with strong poses show consumers the fun side of both the retailer and the designer, making the product and space quickly come alive. As its stores continue to evolve, so does the brand, regularly pushing retail's boundaries. Not only does Harvey Nichols captivate the consumer through its product mix but also through its marketing, visual merchandising, and unforgettable displays.

Another key factor that makes this retailer so successful is the food establishments linked to the Harvey Nichols name, located both in their stores and as freestanding locations. As with other department stores, the introduction of hospitality and food service on-site has proved to be lucrative, keeping customers in the store, shopping longer and hopefully spending more money. Like any other retailer, Harvey Nichols is aware that consumers have a larger number of items per transaction the longer they stay on-site.

"Harvey Nicks, as it is often referred to, has been a leader in the industry for a long time and is proving to be a needed commodity among many shopping districts across the globe."

15 SETTING THE SCENE

Part of the success of Harvey Nichols is that it visually captures its audience through a balance of form and function. Windows, lounges, and performance spaces are always gorgeous to look at while also being consumer-friendly.

Expanding the Harvey Nicks brand

Harvey Nicks, as it is often referred to, has been a leader in the industry for a long time and is proving to be a needed commodity among many shopping districts across the globe. With seven stores located within the UK, a store in Scotland, and shops in exotic destinations, such as Turkey, the United Arab Emirates, Saudi Arabia, and China, Harvey Nichols will soon be located in the luxurious Caucasus region, on the Caspian Sea, in Baku, Azerbaijan. This region is quickly becoming popular among world travelers, and it seems only logical to offer them the premium shopping experience that Harvey Nichols easily provides.

Forward thinking, strong brand strategy, and international expansion have been very successful for the brand. However, a combination of all of its retailing strategies, from management to merchandising, is making it a leader in the specialty department store segment.

15

◀ Case study: Harvey Nichols · Retail consumer markets ▶

36

Chapter 1 summary

This chapter introduced retail as a lucrative system that provides goods and services to consumers for their personal use. After briefly discussing retail's extensive history, we can see how it has evolved and continues to evolve to meet consumer demands. The various retail types for brick and mortar plants was broken down, allowing us to further understand the difference between the wide variety of stores we visit on a regular basis. Traditionally, brick and mortar plants and catalogs have been the primary channels for consumers to procure merchandise, but since the introduction of the Internet, we have seen many channels surface that make it easier to search out cheaper goods across the globe. The use of various retailing approaches will not only offer the consumer greater variety in goods but will also allow the retailer to reach a greater expanse of the global market. It is important to note that despite the various retailer types and the multichannel approaches they use, it is ultimately their goal to drive profits up while keeping the cost of conducting business down.

Questions and discussion points

1. Briefly explain some of the events that caused communities to transition from bartering goods and services to purchasing them from specialty shops.
2. Differentiate the two terms *retailer* and *retailing* and provide examples for both.
3. Define retail typology. What can one learn from understanding the differences between different retailer types?
4. What does the term *brick and mortar* mean? How does it relate to the term *brick and click*?
5. Why do off-price merchants differ from full-price retailers? What retailing approaches do you think off-price merchants can apply to improve the experience for the consumer?
6. The term *multichannel* is slowly being replaced by a new approach referred to as omni-channel. Do you think this is the new approach in retailing? Provide examples to support your opinion.

Exercises

Based on the chapter reading, choose three retailers that do not share a parent company and provide the following:

× Retailer name.
× Retailer type (based on retailer typology discussed earlier in this chapter).
× Date established.
× Corporate offices or headquarters.
× Approximate number of stores.
× Product assortment (i.e., womenswear, menswear, accessories, home goods, etc.).

After providing the information listed above, answer the following questions:

1. Is the retailer using the multichannel approach, and if so, which of the on-site/off-site approaches is it utilizing?
2. Identify one approach for each of your chosen retailers. Do you think this method is successful? Why or why not?
3. What additional approaches would you suggest this retailer use? Are there any you would suggest it cease utilizing?
4. After researching your retailers, provide an overall analysis for how each has evolved in its approaches to accommodate changing consumer needs.

Tip: Locating this information may seem difficult at first, but oftentimes it is available to consumers via the company's website. Look at the bottom of the home page for links to specific company information. You may also choose to visit the store and speak to the store manager or the manager on duty.

2

RETAIL CONSUMER MARKETS

Technology has allowed retailers to gain valuable market share in parts of the world they may not otherwise have had access to. However, they must take into account the demands of the consumer markets in which they offer their goods—looking at the social and psychological characteristics of their markets, just as they would fashion trends. Even on national soil, retailers must conduct extensive market research when faced with situations such as selecting a space to erect a brick and mortar plant, inducting a new label, or relaunching an aging brand. Retailers should not only be knowledgeable in consumer economics but should also understand the factors that influence shopping motives, which stem from both psycho- and socioeconomic situations and affect how their brands are ultimately perceived by the target audience.

1 GLOBAL ACCESS

Many retailers are expanding globally, both in brick and mortar plants and through e-commerce. Regardless of the consumer distribution channel, retailers must be able to cater to the needs of the market they are moving in to. This is something that the Spanish retailer Zara has done by opening numerous stores in Africa, Asia, and the Middle East.

Consumer behavior

What prompts a consumer to make a choice decision on color, brand, or price? How do retailers understand their consumers in an effort to provide them with the best customer satisfaction? These questions only scratch the surface when discussing consumer behaviors and the motives that entice them to shop and purchase the way they do.

Consumer behavior is how individuals or groups select, obtain, and dispose of goods and services to satisfy a specific need. Those that study consumer behavior look at the attributes that relate to consumer psychology, sociology, and economics, and their research primarily looks at the individual or group that selects the product, purchases the product, and/or eventually uses the product (known as the end user).

RETAILERS LOOK AT THREE DIFFERENT SHOPPING MOTIVES WHEN CONSUMERS PURCHASE:

Rational motives: when consumers make purchasing decisions based on analysis that is rational, looking at various elements such as warranties, safety, price, or practicality. Products purchased under this motive are often seen as necessities, such as a coat for winter, organic ingredients in makeup, or comfortable shoes for urban environments.

Emotional motives: those purchasing decisions based on emotional need and/or association with that product or service. These motives are based on a need to feel prestigious or to elevate social status or on an emotionally driven event (e.g., loss of a job, a first date, etc.).

Patronage motives: when consumers purchase goods or services based on their personal preferences, looking at elements such as customer service, product quality, or brand loyalty. A patronage motive is in play, for instance, when consumers continually purchase denim from their favorite brand due to the quality of the product and satisfaction they receive from owning it. While there may be a more popular brand at a cheaper price, they would prefer to stay with the brand they feel most comfortable with.

Keep in mind, consumers usually act on multiple motives when purchasing, typically having a primary and a secondary motive when making the decision on what brand or product to buy.

2 A REASON TO SHOP

Every shopper enters a store or visits a website with purpose, whether it be to satisfy an emotional need or to purchase the most luxurious good her favorite brand is offering during a particular season. Retailers look to further understand their consumers' needs in hopes of growing their target markets while steadily increasing sales revenue.

2

Retailers use information obtained from market researchers so they can better understand their consumers' shopping habits while potentially drawing in new consumers that otherwise have not tested the brand or product previously. To do this, retailers will look at the various motives that cause consumers to shop the way they do, acting and reacting to the various retailing strategies employed by that retailer.

While a retailer has significant control over the way it approaches the consumer, there is no guarantee how the consumer will react. Therefore, the retailer is unable to solidly predict consumers' shopping needs every time. It is important for retailers not only to be aware of their consumers' needs but also the needs of their competition's consumers, allowing them to continually evolve their strategies for capturing new markets while maintaining those that they currently service.

Consumer behavior

Consumer assessment theories

Various theories have been introduced to better understand what makes consumers shop and purchase the way they do. Retailers use information obtained from assessing these theories to analyze consumer shopping and purchasing patterns but, specifically, the decision-making process behind them. Retailers rarely look at one theory in particular but rather use a combination of these theories to find the right mix of retailing strategies to employ within their business. Below are a few of the more significant theories utilized in consumer market research:

× Maslow's hierarchy of needs.
× Consumer perception theory.
× Decision-making model.
× Psychographic segmentation.

Maslow's hierarchy of needs

This theory, first introduced in the mid-twentieth century by American psychologist, Abraham Maslow, looks at how human actions are driven by psychological motivations in an effort to fulfill specific personal needs. Maslow's famous hierarchy of needs pyramid depicts basic human needs (psychological and biological) at the bottom and the need for self-actualization at the top. The theory proposes that people strive to fulfill each need (starting with those listed at the bottom of the pyramid) in order to move toward self-actualization, or personal growth and fulfillment.

Consumer perception theory

Analyzing and assessing the various motives for buying or not buying goods and services, the consumer perception theory looks at how consumers' sensory stimuli (sight, hearing, taste, touch, and smell) are affected by advertising and marketing. This theory defines three perceptions as the reason for purchasing goods:

× Self perception: how a consumer will view himself by values and motivations.
× Price perception: are quality and service justifying the price and is the consumer getting the best price for the chosen good or service?
× Benefit perception: does the consumer need the product or service and can she rationalize purchasing it?

3 DECISION-MAKING MODEL

Consumers make a plethora of decisions when purchasing goods, but the process is always the same. They start by identifying the need or problem, then they establish the criteria. Next they generate alternatives, followed by implementing the decision. This process always ends with a reflection or evaluation of the final decision before the process is repeated or a new need or problem is identified.

Psychographic segmentation

Lifestyle profiling is another way for researchers to study the various attitudes, opinions, and lifestyles of consumers, providing a more defined understanding of a retailer's target market. Looking deeper into consumer lifestyles allows the retailer to better assess why certain audiences are buying into the products and services over others. Ultimately, this may pave the way for entering into new markets in the future or redefining the current one to ensure the retailer is capturing the largest audience in its market segment.

While these and several other theories are out there helping retailers assess, strategize, and implement stronger retailing initiatives, not one can fully explain why consumers shop or purchase the goods that they do. Retailers will continually work with market researchers to find solutions to opportunities that exist in their current models, while hopefully strengthening the successes they currently have within their firm. One of the biggest opportunities for a retailer is truly understanding its demographic, which is discussed further in the next section.

FLOW OF GOODS

3

- IDENTIFY THE PROBLEM
- ESTABLISH/WEIGH DECISION CRITERIA
- GENERATE/EVALUATE ALTERNATIVES
- IMPLEMENT DECISION
- EVALUATE DECISION (REFLECTION)

Consumer demographics

When a retailer opens its doors or website to the public, it will most likely have a specific consumer in mind. This decision will be made by the founding members or the executive committee and will be based on market research conducted during the formation of the firm or as the firm evolves over time. For this retailers look at demographics, or the study of population traits and characteristics.

4

4-6 KNOWING YOUR SHOPPER

No two consumers are physically alike nor do they have the same needs. Identifying their taste preferences and accommodating these while maintaining the company culture can make for a successful retail firm.

5

"When you focus on the consumer, the consumer responds."
Alexander Wang, fashion designer and retailer

Typically, when talking about consumer demographics, we are looking at four specific elements that define a group: age, income, education, and ethnicity. Demographics allow retailers to hone in on the right product to sell each season, choose site locations (discussed later in this chapter), and implement various customer service initiatives that help keep customers loyal while hopefully introducing new consumers to the brand. The consumer a retailer chooses to cater its brand and product to typically sets the tone for the entire company culture.

However, the company culture can be adjusted as markets open, dissipate, or change. Retailers need to ensure they are continually keeping their customer demographics at the forefront of what they do by evaluating the market elements that help to decipher and categorize various consumer groups. Looking at the current customer base, along with the competition's customer base, may help dictate a shift in the customer profile. Similarly, looking at the trading area the store is located in or caters to can provide insight as well.

6

Consumer demographics

Demographics vs. the target audience

Demographics allow a retailer to better understand the wide variety of consumers that frequent its establishments, but it helps to have a specific customer in mind when making decisions that will create the overall look and feel of the brand (i.e., the corporate culture). *Target audience* is a term used to discuss the actual customer the retailer markets and advertises to through the use of consumer behavioral theories, specifically psychographic analysis.

Retailers will look at other defining elements, such as marital status, sexual preferences, and extracurricular activities, honing in on specific consumer lifestyles and attitudes. By doing this, retailers are able to achieve the following:

×   Gain a greater understanding of who their market share is.
×   Establish effective retailing strategies (i.e., marketing, advertising, and visual merchandising).
×   Make seasonal buys that satisfy consumer needs.
×   Generate larger revenue/profit by reacting faster to changes in the consumer market.

Knowing who the consumer is that they are selling to is key to a retailer's success. There are various ways to obtain this information, whether done in-house or by an outside agency.

Mapping the target audience

There are various tools a retailer can use to obtain information regarding its target audience. The easiest way to do this is to hire a consumer research firm that specializes in consumer socioeconomics. While this is a method often employed by larger firms, it can become very costly and may not be a luxury that smaller firms can afford.

7-8 a (× 4): UNDERSTANDING YOUR TARGET MARKET

Paul Rothstein, former Arizona State University professor, discussed the employment of a market research tool called the a (× 4), which allows the researcher to better understand the end-user's lifestyle. This approach looks at the people in their lives (actors), the things they do (activities), the places they go (atmosphere), and the tangible objects they have (artefacts). This research tool can be used with words/phrases or with imagery.

Typically, when the firm is in its incubation phase, most research will be done in-house by the founding members. As the firm grows, it will employ agencies that will help it to collect and analyze demographic data in-house, albeit through customer surveys, zip code/postcode captures, online customer profiles, etc.

For new firms the research process could be as simple as following trends for the product that is intended to be sold. Going to various stores that are considered to be potential competition may give insight into who its target customer may become. Agencies like the National Retail Federation can also provide valuable information for small businesses that may not otherwise be able to afford a specialist.

Each retailer or market research firm will employ the techniques and practices most relevant for capturing the necessary (and vital) information that will best identify its target audience.

a (× 4) MODEL FOR TARGET CONSUMER

boyfriend—Matthew
mom/dad/sister
best friend—Oliver
coworkers at coffee shop
classmates

going to music shows
skateboarding
traveling—backpacking
attending college
squash practice

ACTORS

ACTIVITIES

ATMOSPHERE

ARTEFACTS

college campus—art studio
pubs/coffee houses
outdoors—ocean/mountains
foreign cities—outskirts
Chelsea flat—studio

Vera—gray short-haired cat
skateboard
shoes—Hasbeens/Converse/vintage boots
iPhone—for music and communication
canteen and pocketknife

Site selection and store location

As a retail firm starts to grow and the decision to open a brick and mortar plant (or to invest in corporate offices) is made, a suitable location will need to be identified. Next to having a solid understanding of your consumer demographic, this is the most important decision to make because the wrong site could cause the firm a loss in revenue, immediately or over time.

The most important factor when choosing a site for a retailer's brick and mortar plant is location. Start-ups will often look to save money on this by choosing a cheaper price per square footage, typically in unpopular or rural areas. Retailers, new and established, should conduct a thorough site analysis and carry out research on potential spaces that will help their business to grow over time.

Area characteristics

Fashion brick and mortar operations need to carefully study the proposed location to fully understand its advantages and disadvantages. While some major cities are high trading areas (London, New York, Paris, etc.), others are not. A retailer needs to do a full site analysis for those areas that are lacking the exposure from city dwellers and tourists alike.

Accessibility to the space is also of great importance. Are patrons getting there by foot or using personal or public transportation? Is there ample parking and disabled accessibility (ramps, elevators, etc.)? Has local legislation put laws into place to prevent the acquisition of a site? These are just a few of the questions necessary to ask when doing a site analysis to ensure the chosen area will be visible, sustainable, and profitable over time.

THREE KEY POINTS TO KEEP IN MIND WHEN SELECTING A BRICK AND MORTAR SITE

1. Choose a trading area that best fits the needs of the company. A trading area is the region (state, country, province, etc.) that the retailer will be working in (for instance, London, UK).
2. Explore potential shopping districts within the trading area, looking at key demographic information that may change over time. The shopping district should complement the retail firm and be easily integrated into the district's cultural attributes.
3. Begin visiting exact spaces that will work for your brand. Looking at the various attributes that the site has to offer, such as business neighbors, pedestrian/vehicular traffic, parking, architectural elements, etc., will help you to make the right choice for your brand and product.

9

The most important factor when choosing a site
for a retailer's brick and mortar store is location.

9 FINDING THE
   RIGHT SPACE

At one time, consumers headed
to covered malls to do the
majority of their shopping due
to the large concentration of
similar retail establishments.
Today, many patrons prefer to
shop in city centers due to the
diversity in retailers, resulting
in a requirement to expand
shopping districts.

Site selection and store location

Shopping districts

After determining the trading area, a retailer will want to choose a shopping district—a designated area for retailing. There are various types of shopping districts across the globe, which are typically dictated by the local climate and the region in which they are located.

Years ago, there was a huge move from urban-area shopping districts to suburban, but in recent times, we are starting to see an influx of suburbanites move back to major cities, causing retailers to rethink the opening of satellite stores outside of metropolitan areas. The following information outlines some of the more common types of shopping districts.

Downtown central districts
These used to be barren due to suburban sprawl but have been making a huge resurgence. Located in the centralized area of a major city, a retailer will have its corporate office or the flagship store located here.

Regional malls
Situated in suburban areas, these locations will have satellite stores similar to those in downtown central districts but will typically offer a smaller assortment. Regional malls are often owned by a holding company, which determines who is able to conduct business on the site, allowing for a stronger competitive edge among retailers and less possibility of the oversaturation of like goods.

Mixed-use centers
Mixed-use centers are those that incorporate business, hospitality, and retail, offering a diversified mix of patrons. These centers provide an urban environment, though often they are in suburban areas.

Power centers
Power centers usually comprise twenty or more stores. These centers are where large square footage stores are located and are anchored by big-box discount operations. They are often in suburban areas due to the large amount of square footage needed to build them.

Outlet centers
Housing off-price and factory outlet retail stores, outlet centers are typically far from urban areas, avoiding competition from full-price retailers. They are typically owned by a management company that leases the spaces out to specific retailers.

Site selection

The last decision to make is where the specific site will be located and whether that location will offer the retailer the best chance for long-term success. Looking at specific data gathered through quantitative and qualitative research will reassure the retailer that the best site was chosen and will provide stability and growth for the shop. Data gathered outside of the general demographic studies are:

×   Who and where is my competition?
×   Who are my neighboring tenants?
×   Is there transportation accessibility?
×   Where are the pedestrian and vehicular paths located?
×   Is there entertainment and dining in the area?

A retailer does want some competition in the area, as it can help drive patrons into the store who are shopping for options. However, too much competition may cause a decline in sales due to oversaturation of the market. It is also best not to place your store in an area that does not foster your retail type. For instance, if you open a high-end women's boutique in an area known for its nightlife, this may cause less foot traffic, as people are visiting the area after your store has closed.

There are so many factors that affect the selection of a retail brick and mortar plant, but thorough research and observations can provide valuable insight to making the right long-term decision.

OCCUPANCY CONSIDERATIONS

When a retailer chooses a shopping district, it has two options: to lease or to purchase.

Ownership: If a retailer owns its space outright, it doesn't have to worry about getting permission from landlords to make changes to the exterior or interior of the space. However, it is responsible for all maintenance involved in the upkeep of the space. If, over time, a retailer decides it is not satisfied with the space, there are no leases to break: it can simply lease it out or sell it.

Fixed leases: those leases whereby a retailer pays a set amount each month for a fixed period of time. Lease agreements are set in the beginning, dictating what the landlord is responsible for and what the tenant (retailer) is responsible for.

Graduated leases: those leases whereby the rent costs increase over the duration of the lease. Often, a retailer will pay a percentage increase each year to accommodate inflation. There are also graduated lease agreements whereby a retailer may be asked to pay a monthly rental fee plus a percentage of its sales. While this is a very uncommon practice, it is something to watch out for when signing a lease agreement.

Emerging domestic and international markets

Global expansion in the retail industry is happening faster than we can imagine, with both familiar and unfamiliar brands moving into trading areas across the globe. Retailers previously worried about local competition, but due to the Internet's endless capabilities, consumers are able to find the goods they long for, any time and in any place.

The major fashion trading areas are London, New York, and Paris, but due to retail's global expansion through the Internet, major cities like Tokyo, Abu Dhabi, and Sydney have quickly made their mark with amazing designers and retailers quickly emerging from within. Not only have retailers moved into parts of the globe previously untouched by the industry, but their wholesalers and manufacturers have also expanded into new territories, such as Vietnam, Guatemala, and Indonesia, making the industry much less Westernized and more of an international retail community.

Markets previously untouched by global retailing are now some of the front runners in global retail sales, giving more established markets a run for their money—literally.

National expansion

Retailers today are not only looking at how they can expand outside of national soil but also grow within it. Areas that may have previously been viewed as second- or third-tier markets are now drawing in consumers, creating destination locations of their own. Often, strong design and art communities bring a need for fashion, prompting retailers to investigate expansion in these areas. For example, areas such as Glasgow's Buchanan Street and Vienna's Golden Quarter are quickly emerging as new fashion areas. Stores need not be flagship locations, but they need to offer a selection of the recognized brand to consumers.

Whether it be globally or nationally, retailers are being much more strategic when it comes to expansion, partly due to economic factors, but also because the consumer market is changing from a preference for fast fashion to the need for more sustainable brands and silhouettes, offering quality over quantity.

"The cities of London and Melbourne have such vibrant communities centered around design and innovation. I couldn't think of two better locations for our next West Elm stores."

Jim Brett, president of West Elm, on the global expansion by the US-based retailer

10 CHANGING MARKETS

As we see a greater expansion into the Middle East and Asia, retailers need to devise strategies for successfully capturing these markets, especially if the market is not a familiar one. Western retailers need to be aware of the opportunities that may arise due to culture, customs, or unfamiliar markets.

10

Interview: Tate Ragland — Retail market researcher

///

RÉSUMÉ HIGHLIGHTS

1999–2003

Studied Architecture and Art History at Rice University, Houston, Texas.

2003–2007

Worked as an architect at KPF, in London, UK, before taking a position as an architect for Crate&Barrel, a prominent home goods retailer based in Chicago, Illinois.

2007–2009

Attended Arizona State University, pursuing a Master of Science in Industrial Design, with a focus on design research. Attended ICDHS, design conference in Osaka, Japan, presenting a white paper on sustainability in the media.

2009–2010

Freelanced for various design firms across the US as a design researcher.

2010–Present

Works as a strategic research director for a global brand development and marketing insight consultancy, with a focus on qualitative research and cultural insights.

///

"Deep consumer understanding is critical to brands being able to reach their full potential and remain current and in touch with their customers."

11 ASPECTS OF QUALITATIVE RESEARCH

Working with the client during the qualitative research process enables market researchers to further understand the client's needs, providing greater insight for the brand's growth and development.

Interview: Tate Ragland – Retail market researcher

Q In your opinion, how important is market research for a retailer's success?

A Market research is a critical component of building and maintaining a healthy brand. For brands who are looking to expand into a market, research can save time and money later down the road by identifying potential pitfalls and watch-outs ahead of time. Similarly, established brands with a better understanding of their target consumer can benefit from research by gaining added depth and breadth of knowledge about the constantly changing marketplace and/or changes within the consumer demographic.

Q What is the typical process for collecting consumer market research for retail clients?

A This is determined by the client's central question or primary marketing dilemma. The majority of clients are interested in understanding the customer journey and the different factors involved in leading consumers to make a purchase. In order to get at this, we will typically conduct a series of shopalongs, or accompanied shops, whereby a moderator will spend 1–3 hours with a consumer as they follow their typical shopping routine. This will involve a mixture of observation, direct questioning, and follow-up probing.

Q What are some factors in consumer behavior that you are looking for when conducting your research?

A When doing consumer research it is important to listen and look for not only what the consumer is saying but also the nonverbal cues—in other words, what are they doing that they may or may not be aware of and how can that lend insight into their purchase process.

For instance, a consumer might say that they are not motivated by brand names and labels (because this can have a negative connotation or come off sounding pretentious): however, the moderator might notice that during the shopalong the consumer uses brands as a way of navigating store displays or prioritizing products to explore in further detail. This would then be an important insight to share with the client that might not have been uncovered just by a simple line of questioning.

Q How do you then present this data to the client once you have had the opportunity to analyze and synthesize it?

A Client presentations are always tailored to the needs of the individual audience, but I find that most clients appreciate a PDF or PPT deck that tells a concise story and gives straightforward and clear direction in terms of next steps and ways to action the findings. Most of my clients tend to be brand or marketing managers within their organization and thus bear the responsibility to socializing the outcome of the research within the organization and gaining buy-in from multiple stakeholders.

The more user-friendly and accessible the deliverable from the research vendor, the easier it is on our clients for them to put the insights into practice. Most clients are aware of the exact issues they are facing—what they need from a researcher is a clear strategic plan for overcoming these challenges and moving their business forward.

Q What are some of the challenges your retail clients are facing in the global market today?

A Multichannel marketing continues to be a challenge for retail clients. Finding the right mix of online, print, and in-store marketing campaigns and determining how best to tailor each message to create a multidimensional experience for consumers is difficult for most brands to master.

I also find that many brands have little to no understanding of their target customers and therefore spend lots of wasted time and energy building a message or story without any knowledge of who they are speaking to. Deep consumer understanding is critical to brands being able to reach their full potential and remain current and in touch with their customers.

Case study: Target

One of America's most highly recognizable discount retailers, Target—known for its iconic red bullseye logo—has cultivated a cult following among those who love innovative high-fashion designer–retailer collaborations at affordable, fast-fashion price points. This retailing strategy, coupled with strong design and marketing initiatives, has elevated Target to a status far above its competitors and keeps consumers eagerly anticipating more.

Based in Minneapolis, Minnesota, Target once started as a dry goods store, named appropriately after its founder, George Draper Dayton. As his stores quickly expanded, Dayton Dry Goods Co. soon became known as Dayton Department Store, as Dayton expanded his product assortment and retailing initiatives. After his death and the succession of the company to his son, George N. Draper, the Dayton company began to form strong CSR initiatives and was the first retailer to give five percent of its pretax profits back to communities, setting a standard among the retail industry.

"Success is making ourselves useful in the world, valuable to society, helping in lifting in the level of humanity, so conducting ourselves that when we go the world will be somewhat better of our having lived the brief span of our lives."

George D. Dayton, founder of Dayton Dry Goods Co.

Taking on retail

In the 1960s, Dayton's went from being a family-owned department store to having multiple nationally recognized discount chains, with a new name and logo to set the tone— Target. This was the start of the brand's expansion, first locally and eventually as a successful national chain. At the time, Dayton's had several other brands under its holding company—B. Dalton Bookseller, Dayton Jewellers, and Dayton Dept. Stores, but none grew quite as rapidly as did Target.

After a merger with the J.L. Hudson Company at the end of the decade, the newly formed Dayton-Hudson Corporation added two additional retailers to its mix, creating a stronger, more diverse portfolio. These additions were Mervyn's of California and Marshall Field's of Chicago. While the new brands were nationally recognized, they did not retain the same brand loyalty that Target did, and over time, the Dayton-Hudson Corporation realized this and sold both companies to focus on the strongest member of the family— Target. To reflect the positive growth in the business and create a strong brand, the Dayton-Hudson Corporation later renamed itself to the Target Corporation, which it is known as today.

12 THINKING OUTSIDE THE BOX

Target has embarked on effective initiatives to reinvent the discount operation retailer template, becoming more inner-city friendly and fashion-forward.

Case study: Target

Designer collaborations

One of the most talked about retailing strategies that Target is known for is its continual introduction of designer-retailer collaborations, which have brand loyalists (for both parties) rushing to purchase. Focusing on brand identity, marketing strategy, and design, Target has brought some well-known names into the playing field. Designers such as Michael Graves, Sonia Kashuk, Missoni, and Prabal Gurung, to name but a few, have collaborated on collection pieces that are Target exclusives. This strategy not only introduces the designer but also allows the consumer to have a taste of designer labels at a fraction of the cost.

Recently, Target opened The Shops at Target, a collaboration between Target and shop owners of specialty stores and boutiques (retailer–retailer collaboration). Together, limited-edition collections will be delivered to the public via Target stores, which will allow the small businesses to gain exposure in a large, often intimidating industry. The collections are only for a limited time but allow shop owners to give their unique perspective to the masses, with Target providing the forum to do so. Earlier, we discussed the start of Target's corporate social responsibility initiatives, and this is a prime example of how this company is working with the community to enable it to flourish while remaining profitable and socially conscious.

13 DESIGNING FOR THE MASSES

A retailer that once sold inexpensive, unbranded goods has become a market leader in the art of fashion-retailer collaborations- bringing high-brow fashion to budget-conscious consumers.

Rethinking expansion

Target has been known for its large "white-box" style stores, with large square footages and minimal design. Over the past couple of years, the company has really invested in the visual design of its stores, making them feel less like a discount operation and more like an affordable department store. They tested various models in various shopping districts but have recently moved into a new phase of expansion—exploring downtown and inner-city shopping districts. A recent opening in New York City's Harlem district has revitalized the area and created a more diverse community. Recently, Target opened three stores in downtown areas, appropriately titled City Target, in Seattle, Chicago, and San Francisco, with more stores scheduled to open over the next couple of years. These stores are geared more for the urban shopper and, thanks to extensive market research by the Target team, have catered their retailing strategies appropriately. The stores are built up (not out) to accommodate the small, dense areas. There is more streamlined product that fits the needs of this particular consumer.

With over 1,800 stores in North America, Target recently expanded its tech department to India, which may be the first step to moving this successful retailer into Europe and Asia. Not only is Target a successful retailer with strong CSR initiatives built into its core; it has also been recognized as one of the top US companies to work (and watch out!) for.

13

"Our innovative approach to store design and development allows us to customize the Target model for each location without sacrificing the key tenets that set a Target store apart."

Greg Nations, Senior Creative Manager—Marketing

Chapter 2 summary

Chapter 2 continued to explore the broad spectrum of the
retailing industry, touching on the importance of understanding
consumer demographics and defining a retailer's target audience.
Demographics, while broadly defined by four basic elements—
gender, age, ethnicity, and education—narrows in scope when a
retailer starts to hone in on a specific consumer, which in turn,
can affect the site selection and store location for brick and
mortar stores. Consumer demographics are further quantified
by elements such as salary, location, and marital status, which a
retailer can use to determine marketing campaigns, seasonal
buys, and other consumer-specific retailing tactics. Looking at
emerging markets, both nationally and overseas, may provide a
more defined understanding of where a company should look
when expanding and setting up corporate office roots, which is
discussed further in the next chapter.

Questions and discussion points

1. What are the three consumer shopping motives that
   retailers look at when researching consumer
   behavior? Provide examples for each.
2. Explain the key differences between consumer
   demographics and the target audience.
3. Why is site location considered one of the most
   important decisions a retailer can make? What could
   happen if the wrong site were selected?
4. What are some key points to consider when a retailer
   is researching a site for a brick and mortar plant?
5. How has global expansion changed the way retailers
   view their consumer demographic? Do you think it
   has affected their target audience?
6. Tate Ragland discusses how his clients lack in-depth
   knowledge of their target consumers. Why do you
   think this is? What could his clients do to ensure they
   know who their consumers are?

Exercises

You were just given a lump sum of $100,000 (£61,000) to open your own apparel and accessories shop and need to decide on a location for opening your brick and mortar location. Keeping in mind that you will most likely break even for the first few months that your operation is open, answer the following questions based on the information provided in the text.

1. What type of retail establishment will you choose to open your store with (refer to chapter 1)?
2. What is the general product assortment you would like to carry in your shop? Provide a price point range.
3. What is the general retail concept (i.e., what is the theme of the store)? Provide notes/visuals to reiterate your idea.
4. Select a trading area. Provide detailed research and analysis on your chosen area. How did you come to decide on this area?
5. Choose a shopping district. Define the district and provide justification for your selection. You should include elements such as competition, transportation, entertainment, dining, etc.
6. Provide a synopsis for your overall selection that includes key points from your research and analysis.

1

3

RETAIL CORPORATE OFFICES

Consumers are typically unaware of how retailers provide the services they do, often assuming that most of the work is done in-house, probably during store operating hours. While this may be true for small retail businesses, larger retailers will typically invest in a centralized location that will allow them to facilitate various functions to help support their stores. Whether it is creating ad campaigns for the next seasonal product launch or dealing with a garment's quality issue, home offices take certain pressures off their stores, allowing them to focus on their priorities, which are representing the brand, having strong customer interaction, and, of course, making their prescribed sales goals. It is imperative as the retailer grows and it strives to increase profit percentages each year, that it does so in a socially responsible manner.

1 A ROOM WITH A VIEW

View of dresses displayed at the headquarters of French luxury brand Dior in Paris. Retail and designer offices often provide visitors with museum-like displays to show their successful looks–past, present, and future.

Corporate offices and their role

A retailer's headquarters is the epicenter for providing a multitude of functions that support various areas within the organization—both in the corporate environment and at the store level. Understanding how retailers' home offices support their teams will provide a better understanding of how store environments work when we discuss this further in the next chapter.

The goal of a retailer's home office is to provide support to the various departments within its structure, aiding in the behind the scenes tasks that allow its stores (both physical and digital) to run smoothly and efficiently. To do this, it will typically be structured in a hierarchical format with a president or executive officer at the top and various department heads and employees falling below.

2

CORPORATE STRUCTURE

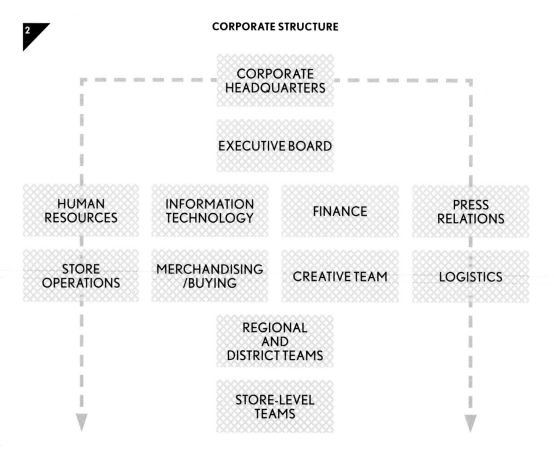

CORPORATE HEADQUARTERS

EXECUTIVE BOARD

HUMAN RESOURCES

INFORMATION TECHNOLOGY

FINANCE

PRESS RELATIONS

STORE OPERATIONS

MERCHANDISING /BUYING

CREATIVE TEAM

LOGISTICS

REGIONAL AND DISTRICT TEAMS

STORE-LEVEL TEAMS

Departments such as human resources, buying, logistics, and PR are handled at the home office, ensuring a consistent image and functionality among stores in the field. Often, a retailer is so large that it invests in regional offices to help facilitate many of these functions. In these cases, the regional offices may conduct business specific to the particular region or area.

For smaller retailers, a corporate headquarters may simply be the shop they are selling from or an owner's or partner's home. However, retailers—large or small—need a centralized location for conducting the important functions necessary to grow a successful business.

SOLUTIONS FOR THE SMALL RETAILER

Like small cities, large corporate offices will typically offer employee dining and recreation and will have a mock-up store on site for testing product or displays or even a manufacturing facility for stronger quality control. But when a small retailer has only a few stores and the need for a corporate office is not necessary (due to size and capital), what does it do?

Typically, small start-up retailers will distribute many of the functions needed to run the business among those who are working there. For instance, a visual merchandiser may also be the buyer, merchandiser, and photographer for the website, or a store manager may also be in charge of logistics, human resources, and multistore operations. Regardless, a space is often designated for these functions to be carried out, whether it is at the store, a rental space, or someone's home. This saves the organization money and allows all employees to stay focused on growing the business.

While having a central corporate office is great for large retailers, the retailers' operations often become disjointed from the everyday workings of their stores, relying on a few individuals to provide feedback to the entire company. Smaller retailers have the advantage of being in their store environment more frequently and, consequently, can adjust their systems more often. Utilizing the various technological resources in the field (Quickbooks, Google SketchUp, and the Internet) will enable small retailers to accommodate rapidly changing markets and allow stronger growth within the industry.

2   TOP DOWN

While each retailer's corporate structure varies, the diagram opposite gives a general idea about how the hierarchical system functions, prior to reaching the store level. Some retailers will combine some departments with like functions, while others will expand based on need.

Corporate offices and their role

3

4

3-6 BEHIND CLOSED DOORS

A retailer's headquarters acts as the central communication hub for the entire corporate community. Departments can work with one another, ensuring consistency before rolling various attributes out at the store level. The corporate location provides financial investors a firsthand look at how the company operates, as seen here in the various pictures taken at the Zara headquarters in Arteixo, Spain.

Corporate offices and their role

Corporate-level departments

Each department within the retailer's organization plays a specific role that directly supports one or more other departments. At the root of an established retail organization are a few departments that need to be further identified:

- × Executive board.
- × Human resources.
- × Merchandising and buying.
- × Creative services.
- × Information technology.
- × Store operations.

These departments carry out some of the most important functions of the company, which directly impact the success of the retailer's stores. Keep in mind that the corporate offices are just as responsible for customer satisfaction as are the stores, and, oftentimes, customer issues will be directed to human resources or a designated customer service department. It is the entire organization's responsibility to drive sales while maintaining strong customer service practices.

Executive board

The members of the executive board are the key players who oversee the daily operation of the entire organization. Their role is to ensure profits to shareholders are being maximized by means of new store development, investor relations, and employee and consumer satisfaction. This group is typically made up of established industry leaders or those whose background can best support the organization in an unbiased fashion. While they are in charge of the company as a whole, they often work directly with human resources, finance, store operations, and press relations.

Human resources

At the heart of any company is a solid human resources department. HR, as it is often called, ensures that company employees adhere to both the company guidelines and legal requirements set forth by the legal system of which it is a part (this could be at a national, state, or territorial level). HR will typically handle various aspects, such as corporate legalities, employee insurance, and training.

Merchandising and buying

Merchandising and buying work hand in hand, partnering to ensure the right seasonal product is purchased, priced, and allocated to the stores or e-commerce distribution sites. While their roles often overlap, the main job function of the buyer is to source the textiles or goods each season and work with the design department to produce the desired silhouette. Merchandisers will then work to create pricing strategies, while continually analyzing business trends (both successful and opportunistic) in an effort to meet goals set forth by the department head or executive committee each season.

Creative services

Most retailers will employ some facet of a creative team, made up of members who are well-versed in the company culture and are able to easily convey this to the consumer via elements such as print or digital media, visual displays, or branded materials. Divisions such as marketing, advertising, and visual merchandising are typically under this department of services, and the people who work here generally have art and design backgrounds.

Information technology

Information technology (IT), is an extremely important department that oversees all of the company's digital information for corporate offices, stores, and the consumer's use. Think of the various web pages or applications you visit on a regular basis and how they differ both visually and operationally. This is what the IT department creates and oversees, in addition to a plethora of other elements, such as employee self-service sites, email usage, and report generators.

Store operations

The stores we shop at need to have someone representing them at a corporate level, and this department ensures that the stores are not only set up to successfully manage their daily operations but also to ensure consistency among stores through product allocation, visuals merchandising and display, customer services, etc. There are various subdepartments that store operations may oversee, which include store design and development, loss prevention, and store logistics.

"In the end, the customer doesn't know or care if you are small or large as an organization. She or he only focuses on the garment hanging on the rail in the store."

Giorgio Armani, fashion designer and retailer

Strategic planning

Planning for a large retail organization takes time, money, and a lot of comprehensive coordination. Goals set by the executive team initiate a series of intricate processes, where each department's success depends on the success of another's. This idea of shared fate, where all stakeholders are working toward the same goal, filters down to the stores, which are just as responsible for helping to achieve the company's overall agenda.

Retailers set their fiscal goals, strategically planning for the next year (as well as five and ten years ahead), hoping to maximize profits while keeping overhead costs down. They will look at previous years' sales numbers and make projections based on market trends and financial analysis. Sales goals specific to each store (and website if applicable) are projected to be achieved daily, monthly, and quarterly. Planning meetings at the corporate level allow department heads to strategically plan for their department associates, to ensure the best course of action to enable their stores and/or website to achieve these goals.

SWOT ANALYSIS

Albert Humphrey presented a strategic planning technique during a Stanford Research Institute convention in the late twentieth century that evaluated a company's strengths, weaknesses, opportunities, and threats (SWOT). The technique identifies internal and external factors that may be favorable or unfavorable when a company is setting out to achieve a particular goal. SWOT analysis enables retailers to make the best possible decisions for current and future projects, as well as potential business opportunities.

Strengths: attributes that give a retailer an advantage over its competition.

Weaknesses: attributes that put a retailer at a disadvantage over its competition.

Opportunities: elements a retailer could use to maximize its profit through exploitation.

Threats: elements that could cause issues, in the present or future, for the retailer.

7 DUNNE AND LUSCH MODEL OF STRATEGIC PLANNING IN RETAIL

A process model, with a linear step approach, the Dunne and Lusch model looks at external forces that may interfere either positively or negatively during the strategic planning process. Being aware of these forces will encourage anticipation and avoidance of specific issues that often occur in the retail industry.

DUNNE AND LUSCH MODEL OF STRATEGIC PLANNING IN RETAIL

competitive environment:
consumer behavior, direct/indirect competition, and supply chain

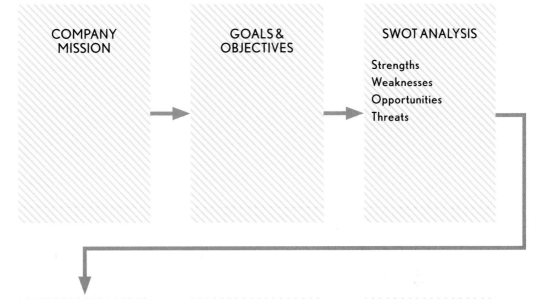

COMPANY
MISSION

GOALS &
OBJECTIVES

SWOT ANALYSIS

Strengths
Weaknesses
Opportunities
Threats

RETAIL MARKETING
STRATEGY

target market
locations
retail mix:
  merchandise pricing
  advertising/promotion
  customer services
  store layout and design

OPERATIONS
MANAGEMENT

buying/distribution
pricing
advertising/promotion
customer services
facilities
stakeholders

HIGH PROFIT
RETAILING

social/legal environment:
socioeconomic environments, legal system, technology, and business ethics

Strategic planning

Forward thinking

Retailers plan far in advance because of the time it takes to solidify elements such as finances, concepts, seasonal buys, and promotional materials. A corporate office that plans far in advance can more easily react to issues that arise in the field, especially in fast fashion, for which consumer needs change dramatically and unexpectedly.

Besides changes in consumer shopping behaviors, other factors could influence future planning. For example, as the cost of petroleum continues to rise, so does the cost of synthetic yarns that are used to make our goods. The acrylic and nylon that a retailer uses to manufacture its goods may need to be substituted in the future for other, more affordable yarns.

Seasonal weather changes may also affect the pricing of the stock on hand. If an unanticipated short winter is followed by a warmer than usual spring, all of the winter coats still at full price may need to be transferred to those store locations still experiencing colder weather, or alternatively the retailer may initiate a markdown of goods.

8

Reacting to business needs to be done strategically, as it can ultimately affect the bottom line and the end goal of a retailer is to turn a profit. Building in markup prices for eventual markdown percentages takes a lot of careful planning. Because buyers purchase goods well in advance of the season they are for, they must think about the periods between seasons and how colors or silhouettes may successfully transition, if they can at all.

The planning process is time consuming and tedious, but those retailers that spend the time and manpower at the front end of the year, as opposed to the back half, will find themselves more organized, less stressed, and able to focus on driving overall sales in stores and online.

8 AHEAD OF THE CURVE

Retailers work diligently to anticipate all possible situations that may present an obstacle for achieving sales goals. Whether it is buying for a future season or planning a markdown schedule to make room for new goods, it is imperative that the planning process accounts for the time-consuming variants, such as delivery dates and window changes.

STRATEGIC PLANNING

Strategic planning in a retail environment is about adapting the resources the firm has to the opportunities and threats that the constantly changing market provides. A retailer needs to anticipate and organize itself in such a way that it is able to reach its goals. The following details are some of the benefits of strategic planning:

× Outlines the overall company goals and agendas.
× Allows the retailer to differentiate itself for the competition.
× Helps the retailer to develop a unique offering to its target market.
× Provides analysis of the current legal and economic environments and helps to forecast future ones.
× Allows for a stronger coordination between the firm's stakeholders (investors, employees, customers, etc.).
× Encourages the anticipation and avoidance of company crises.

Supporting store teams

A retailer's corporate office acts as the brain of the organization, sending frequent communication to each store and aiding it in its daily operations. One of the main reasons a corporate office exists is to lighten many of the back of house functions that would otherwise be left to the owner or store manager to deal with.

Having a centralized location that can oversee various functions helps stores to focus on their number one goal—to make money. Various issues can arise at a store level, and specific departments at the home office can act on behalf of the store facing the issues, while ensuring similar issues do not occur at other locations. The home office also supports the stores by keeping elements such as branding, store design, and employee training consistent.

9 PROMOTIONS FOR STORES

Corporate offices support store teams by providing them with promotional materials each season. Whether it is to inform consumers about new product or about a seasonal sale, home offices provide store teams with materials that will provide a consistent message and ensure that the guidelines set forth by the home office teams are being adhered to.

When stores find themselves dealing with situations beyond their control (or knowledge base), a corporate representative may step in to direct them in the best possible manner for handling the situation. Some areas in which this may be utilized are:

- × Product quality control.
- × Customer service issues.
- × In-store marketing, advertising, and promotions.
- × Employee relations.
- × Brick and mortar plant issues.

9

Areas, districts, and regions

As a retailer begins to expand its business, the interaction between stores and the home office becomes difficult to manage due to the overwhelming number of people that are now part of the organization's mix. Imagine the situation if you are one of two allocators for the company getting phone calls from 15 or more stores regarding inventory needs on a regular basis. This situation can prove to be taxing, especially when each store feels it is the priority. When retailers begin expanding—especially rapidly—they will start to group stores in like markets together, putting their most senior people in charge of these territories. Depending on the number of stores and total sales revenue per store, each year, corporate offices may designate areas, districts, or regions with one representative or a group of representatives acting on behalf of the newly formed territory.

Having stores grouped in this capacity creates a more streamlined communication system between stores and corporate headquarters and allows sister stores to work more closely with one another, supporting each other when necessary. This is a common practice among larger retailers, and the individuals typically in charge of these territories will represent a number of stores in the field prior to moving into home office positions of like-job responsibility.

When stores feel supported by their corporate office, they are able to go about their daily functions with ease, again focusing on driving overall sales. It also allows them to spend the necessary time it takes to train and develop employees or provide elevated customer service, among other things.

Ethics and corporate social responsibility

Retailers, both large and small, must conduct themselves in an ethical manner that will provide them with employee respect and consumer trust. However, ethics are a difficult subject matter, as each individual carries her own set of ethical behaviors, whether it is learned or inherent in her personal character.

Ethics are typically thought of as a set of moral principles that shape the way in which one conducts himself. To further define ethics, especially for a corporate culture, we look at three types—individual, situational, and business ethics.

Individual ethics are those based on moral upbringing, religion, and spirituality and are usually deemed right or wrong by the individual.

Situational ethics are based on events happening at a specific time, whereby one or more parties are left to make a decision on how to best handle what was just experienced. For example, if you see someone getting robbed, do you intervene to help? You are placed in a situation for which you need to make a decision that can affect you both either positively or negatively.

Business ethics are those ethical decisions made in the workplace that will directly affect the company's products, services, and stakeholders. Typically, business ethics are further defined by the company's policies and procedures, which outline acceptable behavior, both on-site and off.

While individual and situational ethics may prompt an employee to react in a specific manner based on an event, she should always keep in mind that during designated work hours, she is representing the company and should adhere to the guidelines that have been put into place to protect both employee and employer.

Ethics in the fashion industry is about more than working with sustainable materials. It is a holistic process—from sourcing to consuming, whereby every stakeholder must be 100% committed to improving the health, safety, and welfare of its industry's members.

Areas of ethical business concern

Retailers partake in a wide range of activities to achieve their goals. Within these activities a wide range of ethical dilemmas can occur:

× Buyer conflict of interest: when personal motivation can cause potential harm to either the employer or employee when acting on behalf of the company.
× Supply chain standards: the minimum ethical behavior that the retailer expects from vendors within the supply chain.
× Internal theft: either being part of the theft or not dealing with a situation when theft from another employee is known.
× Fraternization: dating or habitual socializing of employees by their managers.
× Product misrepresentation: leading consumers to believe their product is better that it is, for example, in terms of quality and sustainability.

Educating employees on the various areas of ethical business concerns will act as a preventive measure to avoid future issues from occurring within the firm.

10 AN INDUSTRY UNITED

Vogue's fashion director Tonne Goodman curates her favorite sustainable items from Barneys New York Co-Op at the Barneys New York celebration for Fashion's Night Out at Barneys New York.

10

Ethics and corporate social responsibility

Corporate social responsibility

One of the more frequent topics discussed in contemporary retail environments today is the idea of corporate social responsibility. Consumers are becoming more aware of the social impact (or lack thereof) that retailers have on both individuals and the environment and are looking for changes in an archaic practice that puts profits before honest business behavior.

Corporate social responsibility (CSR) is the when a company willingly takes responsibility for the actions that directly (and indirectly) affect employees, consumers, and the environment, as well as the community of which it is part. Socially responsible initiatives need to be built into the corporate culture and take time to seamlessly integrate into overall business objectives and plans.

Over time, retailers will build upon each initiative, testing those that work while reformulating those that do not. No two retailers share the same perspective on corporate social responsibility. While one retailer may focus on eco-friendly textiles, another may be working toward fair wages for the factory workers who produce its garments. Each retailer has to decide what it hopes to influence now and in the future, creating a plan that works best for it. It is about identifying the initiative, cultivating it, and then sustaining it over the retailer's life span, looking at and continually addressing those areas that impact the stakeholders, both positively and negatively.

11   BUILDING A BRAND WITH CSR IN MIND

Daniel Silverstein, pictured with John Varvatos, was a contestant on *Fashion Star*, an NBC fashion talent show on US television. Daniel left the show to start his private label utilizing zero-waste technology.

11

12

EXAMPLES OF CSR INITIATIVES

There are a plethora of ways a retailer can strive for a socially responsible organization. Below are a few ideas that have been successful for retailers and have become a standard within the industry:

Philanthropy projects: Many retailers are donating to causes, such as cancer or AIDS research, or partaking in team-building initiatives, such as community service projects. Sometimes, it is not about how much money a retailer can provide but how much time its employees are willing to donate on behalf of the company. This allows employees to build stronger relationships with one another while representing the company in a positive manner.

LEED certified stores: Using the Leadership in Energy and Environmental Design assessment to design new brick and mortar plants or redesign existing ones is a great way for retailers to think sustainably—looking at variables such as natural light, locally sourced materials, low wattage lighting, etc.

Supply chain initiatives: One of the greatest concerns for consumers regarding their favorite retailers is whether the retailers' supply chains are also working toward positive CSR initiatives. Ensuring overseas manufacturers are paying fair wages to employees and that retailers' textile plants are not polluting the water sources are just two key examples of how consumers are looking beyond retailers to ensure all members of the supply chain engage in socially responsible measures.

Retailers should be aware of how their actions can affect so much (and so many), but consumers should also be aware of these actions and make necessary changes in their shopping behavior, forcing retailers to think about the ethical decisions they make in their workplaces, communities, and within the environment.

12 CONSUMER THINKING

Roksanda Ilinčić attends a launch party for the Green Cut at Somerset House, London, which celebrates the best of fashion, film, and sustainability.

Interview: Jackie Mallon — Corporate fashion designer

RÉSUMÉ HIGHLIGHTS

1998

Graduated from the MA Fashion program at Central Saint Martins, London, specializing in womenswear.

1998–2000

Moved to Milan, Italy, and began working as a designer for Moschino, designing for the diffusion label Cheap & Chic.

2000–2006

Worked for Giorgio Armani in Milan, designing across all categories of the Emporio Armani womenswear collection, including lingerie, eveningwear, catwalk showpieces, and fashion accessories.

2006–2007

After moving to the US, became head designer of a Manhattan-based design studio, selling exclusively to Anthropologie, a subsidiary of Urban Outfitters, Inc.

2007–2009

Hired as design director of a New York-based start-up contemporary label with manufacturing partners located in Delhi. Tasked with growing the brand and reaching a greater number of stores while overseeing production operations in India.

2009–2011

Freelanced for wide variety of US-based companies, ranging from Joan & David, designing for its Asian market, to pro golfer Greg Norman's range of women's athletic wear.

2011–Present

Instructor at the Art Institute of New York City in the fashion department and recently published a novel inspired by her experience in the fashion industry, entitled *Silk for the Feed Dogs*.

Q You worked at two prestigious brands, Moschino and Giorgio Armani. What was your research process for understanding the various international markets that you were designing for?

A I was lucky to design for companies who were extremely well established and knew their customers well. In saying that, I was with these companies during a time when the Asian markets were first emerging as a previously untapped customer base and the world was reacting to that. Particular attention was paid to what styles, colors, patterns were appealing to these new customers with money to spend.

We did not design specific collections for any market, but we incorporated their growing needs into each collection. The US was always an important market, not only because of its size, but because, in my opinion, the concept of dressing a woman from office to evening originated with the American career woman and we were always conscious of providing for that.

Q What was your role in the corporate retail structure in comparison to those in buying and merchandising?

A I have had two distinct experiences, the European one and the US one. In Europe, within the companies that I worked for, the buying and merchandising teams worked separately from the design teams and therefore were not greatly involved in our day-to-day work. They prepared sales reports; sometimes we saw them, sometimes we didn't.

We had coordinators who liaised between the two camps, ensuring vital information filtered through. But the general feeling inside European companies, especially ones whose collections culminate in a catwalk show, is that the design department should concentrate on capturing the house's vision for that season and it is the job of the buying/merchandising team to make it work.

There were some compromises and additions to accommodate requests from the buyers/ merchandisers, but generally their job was to successfully represent the designer's message. However in the US, the buying/merchandising teams sit in on design meetings, discuss everything from silhouette to button choice, and this was definitely something I had to get used to when I first arrived. They have a huge say in the design of a garment, the fabric that is chosen, the color of it, how it is trimmed or lined.

Sales reports are a constant presence and are often updated throughout the day. Many successful styles are re-proposed for the following season, and simply the fabric or print is changed in the hope that the customer will continue to buy what they liked before.

Interview: Jackie Mallon – Corporate fashion designer

Q As a designer in a corporate retail setting, how did you balance your personal aesthetic with consumer market preferences?

A It is essential when you work for someone else that you show respect for their vision. Sometimes when you design with restrictions placed upon you, the result is more creative and more surprising than if you had been given free rein to do exactly what you want. A designer who is only interested in pursuing their own agenda has no place in a corporate environment. I would even go so far as to say, a designer like that will become boring very fast, as challenges stoke creativity.

Q When working with overseas manufacturers, what sustainability issues were out of the hands of the designer and retailer? How did you overcome such issues?

A In Europe I worked with companies who manufactured most of their garments in Italy. The Italian factories were well managed and where possible, attempted to abide by sustainable practices. Portions of the collection were made in other parts of the world, and those factories were not monitored or checked.

As designers we tried to source sustainable fabrics to include in each collection, but if something happened to be sustainable but also unique and note-worthy, in appearance or drape, then it stood a better chance of being selected. Sustainability in itself was not enough; it had to be sustainable and beautiful. Fabric mills are realizing this now and are rising to the challenge. Beauty, innovation, and sustainability make for an ideal world.

13 FASHION SKETCHES

Rendered croquis and textile swatches show the designers' points of view for the season, whether they are designing for their own label or the fashion house they are working for.

13

Q How was working with retailers as a freelance designer and creative director different than working for them as an employee?

A As an employee you acclimatize naturally to a company's culture just by showing up for work every day and being immersed, taking on their ways inadvertently. As a freelancer, you have to work harder at this. You need to be extremely organized, good at reading between the lines, and an excellent manager of your own time.

You also need to be easy to get along with, as you do not have the luxury of gaining seniority in a role; you might not even have a designated office, nor do you have the perks and benefits of your employed colleagues. In other words, if it's not working out, you are easily replaced.

Q What advice would you give to students moving into a corporate retail design role upon finishing their studies?

A They must be prepared to be a cog in a system of cogs and wheels, at least initially, which can be hard on the ego. If you have dreams of starting your own label, working within a corporate company can benefit you toward that goal if you approach the experience correctly.

Corporate design experience can certainly be creative, but it is a controlled form of creativity. There are boundaries and conditions and compromises to be reached. All of this makes you a better designer, but some students are not cut out for it directly out of school. There is so much more to a successful business than designing a cool product.

"A designer who is only interested in pursuing their own agenda has no place in a corporate environment. I would even go so far as to say, a designer like that will become boring very fast, as challenges stoke creativity."

Case study: American Apparel

In 1989, Canadian-born Dov Charney founded a company that was rooted in strong corporate social responsibility and the idea that the cotton T-shirt was an American icon. Dov worked diligently to nurture an idea that started in his dorm room and has now grown into one of the most recognized and respected retail establishments based in the US, perfectly named— American Apparel.

Based in downtown Los Angeles, California, American Apparel has built a reputation among a young, hipster cult following who cannot get enough of the wide assortment of fashion basics that seem to mimic seventies and eighties aerobic fashions. Not only is its apparel unmistakable, but so are the risqué (often raunchy) marketing ads that set American Apparel apart from its competitors. There are no super models, no professional actors—just employees posing in the basic color knitwear they so proudly manufacture in the vertically integrated facilities that also house company departments, such as creative services and human resources. This truly is a one-stop corporate shop, which is causing many fast-fashion companies to rethink the retailing model.

"America doesn't need another faceless, institutional apparel company. They need an apparel company that gets it and does it right."

Dov Charney, founder and CEO of American Apparel

Vertically integrated

There are very few retail companies today that are vertically integrated, meaning they manufacture and sell their goods both wholesale and retail. With the largest sewing factory in North America, American Apparel doesn't outsource its sewing overseas like its competition, which relies on low-cost labor to turn a larger profit. Labeling itself, "sweatshop-free," American Apparel works hard to ensure its garment workers get paid a fair minimum wage—50 times more than other fashion manufacturing companies. Owning and operating its own dye houses and knitting facilities aids in this gesture, while keeping production seamlessly run by home office management.

On top of paying fair wages, it offers insurance benefits to all its employees as well as subsidized public transportation, lunches, and an on-site masseuse. Known for being an outspoken advocate for immigration, American Apparel offers ESL classes as well. In the field, employees get well-appointed discounts, and transparency in the company means they are able to voice concerns and openly discuss issues they may feel strongly about.

14 NOT JUST AMERICAN APPAREL

American Apparel began in the Los Angeles market but has quickly spread its wings to overseas markets. Being vertically integrated, specifically selling wholesale, allows it to have a presence not only in its stores but in many other retailers' stores around the world.

14

Case study: American Apparel

Wholesale vs. retail

American Apparel is a great example of how companies can separate the wholesale business from the retail. Many retailers utilize American Apparel goods for their own private labels, allowing US-produced goods to be sold in larger quantities around the globe. Doing this keeps production levels high, in turn keeping costs down for the retail side of the American Apparel business. This also creates stronger competition for those goods that consumers feel are better quality and have a more transparent manufacturing story. The retail side competes with fast-fashion retailers that sell basics (Gap, Old Navy, Express, etc.) and that source their manufacturing process in underdeveloped nations, sacrificing quality in the long run. Operating in over 18 countries, American Apparel has a lot of production to keep up with, producing over one million garments each week.

15 CONTROVERSIAL CAMPAIGNING

One of the most recognizable American Apparel retailing attributes is its marketing campaigns, which use raw photography and jaw-dropping concepts to get consumers' attention.

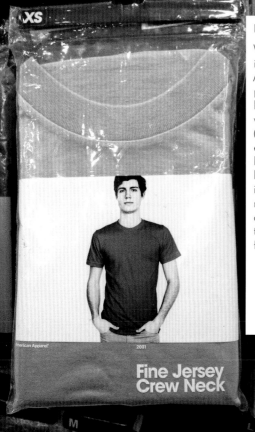

Deep-rooted CSR

We are well aware of the positive impact that a vertically integrated retail system offers communities, but for American Apparel, it doesn't stop there. A company that prides itself on diversity seeks out individuals who can bring impact (and controversy) to the company. With well-known support for the overruling of Proposition 8 (a California state constitutional amendment that eliminated the rights of same-sex couples to marry) and by creating ad campaigns to "Legalize LA," in hopes of bringing awareness to US citizens with regard to immigration reform, American Apparel has looked to redefine how retail companies and consumers view corporate social responsibility. It has worked hard to set the bar for established retailers, while creating a norm for start-ups.

"Commerce is the key driver toward societal change. If everyone that produces the goods the world consumes starts concerning themselves with sustainable, low-impact practices, the world will change."

Dov Charney, founder and CEO of American Apparel

Chapter 3 summary

Corporate offices work to ensure that a consistent message is
created among stores in the field while strategically planning
a wide range of tasks each season that enable solid growth to
occur. Smaller retailers don't always have the financial
backing to establish a home office space but still deal with
many of the same issues that larger retailers must face on a
daily basis, usually doing so from the store environment.
Larger retailers create various home office departments to
oversee functions within the organization and, as they
continue to grow, create territories within the field that group
similar markets together—hoping to make communication
between the home office and stores more streamlined.
Retailers, small and large, need to be aware of how their
organizations impact both people and the planet, to work to
keep a socially responsible approach to retailing.

Questions and discussion points

1. What are some of the ways corporate offices can
   support stores within the field?
2. Briefly discuss a retailer's corporate hierarchy and
   why this business structure is necessary.
3. Identify two departments in a retailer's corporate
   office. How might these two departments support
   each other's workload?
4. Define SWOT and explain its importance for a
   retailer's overall strategic plan.
5. What is corporate social responsibility? Do you think
   contemporary retailers do a good job of instilling this
   in their corporate culture? Provide examples to
   support your argument.
6. Buyers are faced with a multitude of ethical decisions
   to make. Thinking about the various issues that occur
   in the manufacturing industry, provide three ethical
   issues that a buyer may be faced with in dealing with
   this part of the supply chain.

Exercises

Corporate social responsibility has a different meaning for each retailer. Choose two retailers, one that you shop at on a regular basis and one that you don't, but that has a similar target market (e.g., Gucci and Prada). Thoroughly research both retailers, looking at their corporate websites, reading articles published about them, and visiting store locations and speaking with store teams. From your research, answer the following questions:

1. What are some of the various retailing activities that both retailers are using that fall under the idea of corporate social responsibility. For example, one retailer may provide an on-site textile recycling bin in its stores, while the other may print all of its marketing on recycled paper with soy-based inks. Provide a minimum of three examples for each.
2. Does one of your retailers seem to be more established in its CSR initiatives than the other? Why do you think this may be?
3. Identify one CSR initiative for each retailer that in your opinion is a success. Then, identify one opportunity for each retailer. Explain your answers.
4. As CSR initiatives become more transparent in the retail industry, what are some of the ways you think retailers could build this into their strategic plans and how would it benefit their overall sales goals?

DSQUARED
FILIPPA K
J.BRAND
LEBOR GABALA
MIHARA YASUHIRO
MM6 MARTIN MARGIELA
N,D,C
OPENING CEREMON
P.A.R.O.S.H.
RING
SUN68
TOM FORD
VEJA

NOTÉNOM
& WOMEN

1

STORE MANAGEMENT

4

As consumers pass shop windows, deciding whether to venture in, store teams eagerly wait inside, completing the daily routines involved in running complex fashion brick and mortar plants. From store opening to closing, management personnel oversee a plethora of tasks that aid them in achieving the daily sales goal set forth by the store manager and corporate offices. These tasks are the overall responsibility of the store manager but are overseen by various management positions set up at the store level to ensure a smooth execution of the brand's designated retailing strategies. In-store human resources, training, and inventory control measures are just a few of the back of house functions that are key for running a successful retail store in a contemporary retail environment.

1 ENTICING THE CUSTOMER

Storefronts need to draw customers in with strong brand representation, to allow sales teams inside to provide the customer service necessary to make the final sale. Established retailers, such as NOTÉNOM, are fully aware of the importance of brand, as seen in this El Born district store, located in Barcelona, Spain.

Store management and the back of house

Store management teams are a group of players that oversee the daily operations of a brand's brick and mortar plant, acting as the liaison between corporate offices and the consumer. A great deal of responsibility is placed on this team, especially the store manager (sometimes called director), who needs to strategically staff, train, and manage all employees—ensuring that everyone commits to maintaining the brand's image while actively contributing to those retailing strategies that will enable the store to reach its prescribed financial goals.

Retail stores are complex systems that typically have a hierarchical structure, with the store manager at the top and sales associates at the bottom in the chain of command. Under the direction of the store manager, department managers are hired to oversee a more narrow scope of the overall store responsibilities, helping the store manager to facilitate company direction, which is handed down from a corporate level.

MANAGERIAL ROLES

Though titles differ from retailer to retailer, managers across the industry hold similar job responsibilities. Below is a list of the various management roles often employed within retail stores:

- × **Store manager:** the director of the store who wears many hats to effectively run a brick and mortar plant. Usually, the store manager is the most senior position, training and developing department managers to company standards.
- × **Operations/facilities manager:** oversees plant maintenance issues, such as cleaning, electrical, and plumbing, acts as the store representative to outside contractors, and ensures all supplies are ordered for the store.
- × **Hiring manager:** the direct link to corporate offices for recruiting employees within the store. This person ensures that employee files are complete and employees are consistently trained and developed.

- × **Apparel/accessories department managers:** those managers in charge of specific departments within the store, such as womenswear, menswear, or accessories. These managers typically oversee the more narrow scope of needs within their departments and communicate successes and opportunities, such as product, talent, etc., to the store manager.
- × **Receiving manager:** takes in all daily shipments as well as facilitates those shipments leaving the store. Main responsibilities include store logistics, back of house inventory controls, and shipment processing.
- × **Visual manager:** typically works in conjunction with the store manager to ensure all visual requirements made by corporate offices are implemented and maintained. Utilizes a combination of both merchandising and visual merchandising strategies that help to convey the overall brand aesthetic to consumers.

2

In tandem with the store manager, department managers share the responsibility for store opening and closing, employee training and development, seasonal floor set execution (discussed further in chapter 5), and various other tasks that are required to ensure the store runs effectively and efficiently each day. The term *back of house* is used to describe the areas of the store that shoppers cannot see, such as the back stock, manager's office, and employee break rooms. This is where store teams perform the retailing functions that are typically invisible to customers. Back-of-house functions are carried out by every store employee and enable the "front of house," or the actual shop sales floor, to remain consumer-friendly.

2 SHARED FATE

Managers work together to ensure the back of house functions are completed each week, which in turn allows the shop floor to run more effectively. Whether it is size auditing, ordering supplies, or hiring new employees, all managers actively support each other, often taking on responsibilities that do not form part of their job description.

Store management and the back of house

Back of house

As mentioned previously, the back of house are those areas of the store that shoppers do not have direct access to. Break rooms, back stocks, and management offices are spaces that hold vital company information (and product) that needs to be secured from the nonemployed. These strict access areas are designated to facilitate some of the following functions:

× Provide a safe and secure area to count cash and process customer payments, returns, and discounts, as well as perform other tasks that need to be completed securely.
× Offer store teams a break area to eat, relax, and socialize away from the sales floor.
× Process and store shipments when new and replenished goods are sent to the store.
× Provide areas for company policies and documents, such as current regulations or local and federal legislation, to be visible and accessible to all employees.
× Provide storage for house fixtures, props, mannequins, and other visual display units not used on a frequent basis.

Retailers typically forbid any non-employee from entering the back of house spaces unless escorted by a manager. Due to the sensitive materials displayed throughout and the need for strict inventory control measures in these spaces, rarely will any managers provide access to the back of house unless they are interviewing potential talent for the store.

Daily routines

Managers spend a great deal of time in the back of house, planning and organizing employee schedules based on the needs of the store and direction passed down from corporate offices. They need to look at payroll calculations, employee availability, company promotions, holidays, and a plethora of other factors that may affect the shop's daily routine.

7:00 AM

MORNING SHIFT

× Opening manager lets in staff.
× Closing notes reviewed by opening team and any immediate issues are taken care of.
× Cleaning routine begins and stock replenishment occurs.
× Opening manager reviews daily schedule and provides team with daily sales goals.
× Department directives are completed and customer service becomes the priority.

MIDDAY SHIFT I

× Midday shift I team relieves morning shift team for breaks.
× As teams return from break, midday shift teams help to complete unfinished projects.
× Focus becomes more customer-centered in preparation for peak selling times.

Though retailers' daily routines vary based on their retail type, most adhere to a fairly similar plan for opening and closing the shop doors. Morning teams are put in place to clean and replenish the goods that have sold down, hitting key areas, such as zone entries, displays, and points of purchase. Without customers in the store, they can freely enter and exit back of house spaces, easily getting product in and out of back stocks. They thoroughly clean the store, focusing on customer service-oriented areas, such as fitting rooms and cashwraps (cash desks).

3 SHIFT RESPONSIBILITIES

There are several shifts that employees may be scheduled for, with many overlapping and starting before the store opens or after it closes. Each shift entails specific tasks and responsibilities that keep the shop floor running smoothly for customers.

Midday teams are scheduled to relieve morning teams for breaks as well as to focus on customer service to drive midday sales. Minimal restocking occurs on this shift, again so teams can focus on driving sales for the day. When closing teams arrive, they continue strong customer service initiatives and focus on sales floor recovery from an evening of increased customer foot traffic. These team members will reorganize the sales floor, getting it to a position whereby the store could successfully open (and function) the next morning should any opening issues occur.

All of this occurs as the management staff continually moves to and from the back of house to take conference calls, interview potential employees, carry out inventory counts, and perform a number of other required duties that must be completed out of the customers' sight, so not to distract them from making purchases.

3

MIDDAY SHIFT II

- × Midday shift II team relieves midday shift I team for breaks.
- × All projects are cleaned up except where inventory replenishment is necessary for making daily sales goals.
- × Heavy focus on engaging the customer at store entry, sales floor, fitting rooms, and point of sale.
- × No projects occur at this time.

NIGHT SHIFT

- × Closing team works to exceed daily sales goal through enhanced customer service.
- × Closing routine begins—counting down registers and cleaning and organizing fitting rooms and the cashwrap (cash desk).
- × Spot filling occurs if necessary, but focus is on floor recovery (refolding/hanging and display product sell-off).
- × Managers make closing notes for opening teams and close the store.

10:00 PM

Employee management

One of the most challenging functions of running a store is coordinating the many individuals who make up the store team. From managers to sales associates, each team member has a specific duty that directly contributes to the success of the store and whose role could negatively affect the entire day if not properly managed. Employee success starts when the job offer is accepted.

Interviewing and employee files

Managing a store's employees is no easy task. Every manager must provide some assistance to ensure that the store teams are properly trained, are working efficiently, and, most importantly, are appreciated. From the interview to the hire date and throughout the duration of their employment with the company, managers partake in a number of tasks necessary to complete an employee's file, ensuring it is continually audited for company and local and federal mandate compliance.

**4-5 INTERVIEWING
FOR TALENT**

If the store is small enough, a manager may conduct background and reference checks on the sales floor during downtime. Sometimes, if a large number of associates are needed for a store or group of stores, retailers may hold recruiting sessions, at which interested candidates can fill out applications and sit in on group interviews.

When a potential employee is invited to an interview he is asked to bring his résumé (CV) and a completed job application (filled out in its entirety) to give to the interviewing manager. These are the first two documents that make up an employee file, kept in the store for the duration of employment. If the potential candidate is hired, managers will add those items required by local and federal laws (copy of identification card, legal right to work documentation, tax information, etc.) and company requirements, such as handbook sign-off sheets and offer letters, into his file.

An employee's folder stays in the store while the employee is actively employed and from three to seven years if the employee is not, depending on employment laws for that area.

Employee management

Group interviews

Depending on the season and number of talent the store needs to recruit, an interviewing manager may choose to do one-on-one interviews or bring a number of potential candidates in for a group interview. Group interviews are becoming a norm in the industry, allowing interviewing managers to easily distinguish personality types and individual work ethics, as well as to gauge how candidates will work in group settings. Identifying these attributes allows interviewing managers to choose candidates who best fit within the company culture and will be strong team players.

Training and developing

An associate is only as good as the person who trains her. Recognizing this, many retailers are investing heavily in training modules for employees so customer interaction and company image are consistent across retailers with multiple stores. Training is delivered in a variety of formats, all of which are best learned from utilizing a combination of methods:

× Role-playing.
× Seasoned staff shadowing.
× Interactive digital media.
× Employee handbooks and videos.
× Employee evaluations.

THE HIRING PROCESS

| Fill out application/ submit résumé | Preliminary interview | Reference check/ testing | Second/final interview | Decision making |

Training programs are different for each retailer, but most retailers include some facet of their organizations' missions, goals, and procedures. It is important to understand that training is not necessarily about new training but about continued training throughout the duration of employment, which is provided for all levels of the organization that are vital to the retailer's success.

Developing employees is a continuing process for managers, as this provides the necessary training to move sales staff into leadership roles. Across the board, a retail manager's greatest opportunity is to provide the foundation for growth within an associate's position, allowing her the opportunity to have a hands-on approach to the various retailing strategies that a store engages in.

It is easy for an associate to get lost on the sales floor, so it is imperative that managers have solid development plans for their staff—setting attainable goals and providing consistent feedback.

INTERNAL VS. EXTERNAL CANDIDATES

Hiring from within or looking for talent outside the company has its pros and cons. Below are a few key points for each:

Internal
- × Familiar with company culture.
- × Company has already invested in training and development.
- × Motivates employees to work hard to get promoted.
- × May become stagnant or disgruntled, may lack new ideas.

External
- × Brings a new set of ideas and fresh set of eyes to the store.
- × Eagerness to learn.
- × Unfamiliar with company culture and practices.
- × Higher turnover rates.

6 THE HIRING PROCESS

Each phase of the hiring process is important and necessary to ensure the right candidate is chosen and that he will be able to fulfill the requirements of the job.

Store logistics

Store teams need to have complete control over shop operations, particularly in relation to the logistical systems that enable stores to function efficiently and at full capacity. From taking in inventory to devising pricing strategies, store teams could easily spend their entire shifts tending to those tasks that do not include directly servicing customers. It is for this reason that store operations are best facilitated through consistent communication between the stores, corporate offices, and third-party vendors.

Logistics in a retail setting pertain to the coordination and management of the resources that flow from the point of origin to the end user for consumption. The effective flow of information is critical for both tangible and intangible goods. The logistics in place are organized and managed by all parties involved, although this is not always done properly (or successfully). It is imperative for all those involved in the logistical process to remain proactive, always anticipating and being ready to react to hiccups in the system.

RETAIL LOGISTICS

Logistics is the management of both tangible and intangible goods that stores engage in on a daily basis:

Tangible
× Shipping and receiving of inventory and supplies.
× Inventory control measures.
× Merchandise.

Intangible
× Flow of information from corporate office to stores (i.e., sales reports, inventory lists, or price adjustments).
× Time allocated to projects.
× Exchange of currency via credit and debit transactions.

7 RETAIL LOGISTICS MANAGEMENT MODEL

From raw goods to consumption, retailers continually manage the flow of goods and services from suppliers to shoppers or through reverse logistics-the flow of goods and information from consumers back to retailers. This model works concurrently with the supply chain system, as discussed in chapter 1.

RETAIL LOGISTICS MANAGEMENT MODEL

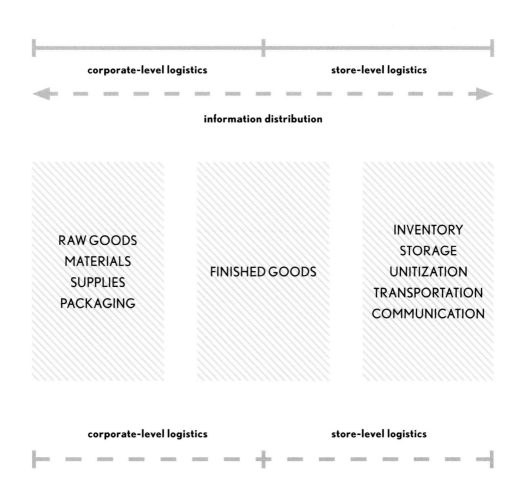

corporate-level logistics   store-level logistics

information distribution

RAW GOODS
MATERIALS
SUPPLIES
PACKAGING

FINISHED GOODS

INVENTORY
STORAGE
UNITIZATION
TRANSPORTATION
COMMUNICATION

corporate-level logistics   store-level logistics

Store logistics

Distribution

In the short term, store logistics allow retailers to execute their daily routines in a seamless fashion. However, in the long term, they allow retailers to grow within the market—often enabling them to enter into national or global communities previously untouched by their brands. Of the various store logistics segments, distribution, communication, and value-added services are the most complex, needing constant evaluation for the retailer to remain successful.

The distribution of goods is an incredibly important task, especially due to the large presence of e-commerce retailers and simplified shipping processes used in contemporary retailing. Nowadays, retailers can quickly replenish store inventory levels, easily accept customer returns, or directly ship to the consumer from their warehouses (or even the suppliers' warehouses) through such means as the Internet or personal digital assistants (PDAs) (discussed further in chapter 6).

Technological advances simplify the distribution system, enabling a quicker turnaround time for both the retailer and the consumer.

8

Communication

A retailer's IT department or information technology services is a vital part of its communication methods, which can easily cause an increase or decline in overall sales. Think about being on the Internet or telephone and how impatient you can become during the slow processing of a credit card payment or a long wait on hold. This can quickly convince consumers that they don't need the item and prompt them to seek out another retailer who can provide them with much faster service. Aside from IT support between the retailer and the consumer, stores have to be able to easily communicate between each other and their corporate offices for such issues as product updates or changes in company policy.

Other communication systems may be put into place for specialized areas, such as company banking, supplier—vendor orders, direct mail, and social media.

9

Value-added services

Value-added services are those areas in the logistics process that are product focused and help to generate sales in a more efficient manner:

× Ticketing of goods.
× Packaging of product.
× Labeling of the box after unitization.
× Point of purchase methods.

Logistics can aid a retailer's success in many ways and should be continually assessed to ensure the strategies employed are the most cost effective and efficient.

8-9 LOGISTICS CHANNELS

Distribution, communication, and value-added services are some of the most crucial concerns for retailers. These systems not only help drive revenue for the company and make employee tasks easier but will inevitably affect consumer views on the company if the systems are weak and inefficient.

Merchandise controls and loss prevention

Loss prevention (LP) is a constant battle for retailers, forcing them to continually deal with both internal and external factors that can ultimately cut into a store's overall profit and drive the cost of company retailing tactics up. Loss prevention initiatives are put into place to prevent this loss from being passed on to consumers through price increases or sacrificing quality.

While loss prevention is the actual act of deterring theft within a store, the term *shrink* is used to identify the actual loss. Shrink rate is a percentage of the store's total monetary sales. For instance, if a store made $10,000 (£6,000) in sales for the day and it was determined in the same day that $500 (£300) in product was lost, then the day's shrink rate is $500 (£300) ÷ $10,000 (£6,000) = 0.05 × 100 = 5.0%, the percentage of the daily sales that was lost due to theft or human error. Typically, a retailer will not review shrink rates daily but will make a note of what was potentially lost each day and then compare those numbers at the end of the year when store inventory is checked against corporate reports.

Shrink happens for various reasons, but most commonly, it is identified as occurring from the following three areas:

× Internal theft: loss due to employee theft at both the store and corporate level or loss due to theft occurring from logistics channels, such as supply or distribution.
× External theft: loss occurring from shoplifting or Internet/banking fraud.
× Paperwork errors: errors occurring due to internal or external forces, such as accidentally miscounting shipment deliveries or mismarking prices.

Many retailers are more concerned about the actual loss than they are about the way in which the shrink occurred. Knowing the cause of shrink is important because it allows retailers to take the necessary measures to prevent future loss from occurring.

"Shrinkage is the single greatest threat to profitability in our industry."
Alasdair McKichan, president, Retail Council of Canada

10 INTERNAL THEFT

Retailers continually battle internal theft, which is sometimes more difficult to control than paperwork or external loss. Associates often feel that they are underpaid and will help themselves to product to feel compensated accordingly. Another issue is what many retailers refer to as "sweethearting"–when associates working cash registers do not ring up the purchase in its entirety or turn a blind eye to friends who shoplift for them.

Merchandise controls and loss prevention

11

MERCHANDISE DISTRIBUTION

Retailers, regardless of size, need to establish inventory control measures for shipping and receiving merchandise to stores—especially to ensure they are receiving the merchandise that is scheduled for delivery on the invoice. There are several ways in which they do this:

× **In-house distribution:** Goods are sent directly to stores, and store teams check inventory against the shipping invoices.
× **Centralized receiving areas:** Retailers have goods sent to a central location, and after the central location checks quantities against invoices, it distributes the goods to the store levels.
× **Regional or national receiving areas:** Warehouses in various regions or in one central area receive merchandise and then distribute it to centralized receiving areas.

11-12 DETERRING POTENTIAL THEFT

Most retailers use a combination of theft deterrents to prevent shoplifting. Enhanced customer service, clothing sensors, or hired security are some of the most common methods utilized in stores.

Theft deterrents

Retailers are constantly searching for new ways to deter theft at the store level, and they often look to technology as a means for doing so. However, as fast as they discover new technology to do this, shoplifters discover ways around it. The following methods are used by retailers to deter theft:

×   Quantity checking: counting actual inventory against inventory reports or piece counting received inventory against invoices.
×   Electronic article surveillance: systems used to detect merchandise that has been fitted with a magnetic device that sets off an alarm system when passed through. This is the most common technological system utilized.
×   Video surveillance cameras: set around the store and a live feed, which is videotaped, streams into the main offices.
×   Employee screening process: carrying out thorough background checks.
×   Fitting room controls: constantly monitoring the fitting room and thoroughly cleaning and scanning for hard tags or pins, as well as constantly checking in with customers.

Retailers will consistently agree that the best deterrent for shoplifting is customer service. Engaging customers will show them you are aware of their presence and may prevent them from seizing the opportunity to steal.

12

Interview: Shana Tabor — Vertically integrated retailer

RÉSUMÉ HIGHLIGHTS

1996–1999

Studied jewelry design at the Fashion Institute of Technology (FIT) in New York City, followed by a one-year intensive study program in accessory design also at FIT.

1999–2002

Worked in freelance design and merchandising for various mass-market jewelry and accessory companies in New York, specializing in licensing and private label goods.

2002–2004

Took on a role as assistant designer for high-end costume jewelry company, Roxanne Assoulin.

2005–Present

Launched In God We Trust (IGWT), a multifaceted brand, comprising both men's and women's clothing, jewelry, and accessories, as well as private label collections, focusing on US-manufactured goods. Opened three brick and mortar locations under the IGWT brand (all in New York) and an e-commerce site. Launched bridal jewelry collection, "Let's Get Serious," consisting of custom-made commitment and wedding bands.

13

Q What is the story behind the brand name In God We Trust?

A The name was a general comment on American consumerism and the value we place on objects.

Q As a vertically integrated retailer, how do you handle the demands of manufacturer, wholesaler, and retailer?

A We currently wholesale only our jewelry. Our jewelry is always made to order, so as long as we have the manpower in our studio we are good to go. Jewelry (for us) is very different than apparel. Our resale customer will reorder frequently and consistently. We don't have to wait for a new season to launch a collection. Apparel—we supply only our own stores, so we watch our numbers of previous seasons' sell-through and watch our production budget. Since we manufacture smaller runs either in-house or locally, we can have a quick response and fill in holes if we need more or new merchandise.

Q How do you determine the right product mix within your store since you carry both private and national brands?

A We are carrying less and less national brands and other brands in general.

We are trying to focus on making our own products and exclusively offering them in our own locations. We buy into brands that offer categories that are difficult or too expensive for us to produce in the state—machine/handknits, small leather goods, shoes, etc.

"There is nothing like creating a store environment—the Web hasn't quite figured that part out yet."

13 BRICK WALLS AND EXPOSED PIPES
Many shop owners use existing architecture within their spaces as part of their visual display, which is not only cost effective but often indigenous to the vernacular of many historical shopping districts.

Interview: Shana Tabor — Vertically integrated retailer

Q **What do you look for when hiring talent for your brick and mortar store?**

A We are always looking for an "A" game. Sweet, well-mannered, yet witty, and interesting people. I think our staff in our stores or studio takes a real ownership and pride in our company. It makes a huge difference to offer someone a sense of integrity.

Q **How do you keep consumers returning to the shop in the digital age of e-commerce?**

A I'm hoping our amazing staff, customer service, and great selection of products!

Q **How do your brick and mortar stores facilitate conversion on the IGWT website?**

A We try as much as possible to get our store staff to involve our customers. For example, pictures of people in our clothes or even of their cute pets. Social media has proven to be important, and our customers are very responsive. We also include all of our staff on our website. We are a team!

Q **Where do you see the greatest growth in your business over the next five years: brick and mortar or e-commerce?**

A I could answer all of the above, but this is a matter of how much energy we personally have to make the brick and mortar grow. It takes a lot more overhead (as well as headache) to run a physical location. However, there is nothing like creating a store environment—the Web hasn't quite figured that part out yet.

14 OUT-STOCKING GOODS
Carefully curated displays create an enticing shopping experience for the consumer, while housing product on the sales floor, and thus alleviating the need for back stock and the possibility of a missed sale.

Case study: All Saints

At first glance, you cannot help but sit in wonder at the wall of vintage Singer sewing machines that make up the entry windows of many All Saints stores. This signature display is the start of the British-based retailer's visual cues that draw consumers in to experience what many have referred to as 'rock 'n' roll' chic.

Founded in 1994, All Saints began as a menswear wholesaler, providing high quality goods to upscale department stores, such as Harrods and Harvey Nichols. The brand was introduced by designer Stuart Trevor, who strategically launched his first store on November 1, 1997 (All Saints' Day). Trevor, along with Kait Bolongaro (the original womenswear designer), introduced womenswear to their Foubert Place store in London, one year later. All Saints has since grown to include both men's and women's accessories, shoes, and childrenswear.

There are currently over 100 stores worldwide and over 30 concessions at various other retailers. To manage this large presence across the globe, All Saints has its headquarters in London, UK, and has various regional offices in the US, Asia, Middle East, and Europe. Having this large reach enables it to continually stay in tune with its markets, providing consumers with the vintage-industrial aesthetic to which they are accustomed.

"I think it's really important to immerse yourself in the market–study the latest trends, find out what's out there, and be original–but make sure it's also commercially viable."

Stuart Trevor, All Saints co-founder

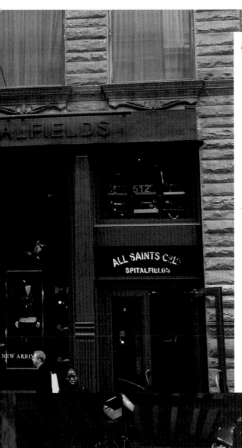

An aesthetic to remember

If customers do not remember the vintage sewing machine window display that seems to pay homage to the manufacturing district where All Saints began (London's historic Spitalfields), then they should surely remember the beautiful mix of raw materials that engulf the interior spaces, further reiterating the All Saints brand. Raw wood, brick-clad walls, and fixtures repurposed from industrial steel machinery are the highly textural surfaces that complement the muted mix of product, skillfully merchandised throughout the store.

There is little change aesthetically between the women's and men's sections, only to be differentiated by means of silhouette and product placement. Architectural elements act as a means for discovering both current- and last-season's goods spread throughout the shop floor, carefully curated to meet consumer demand. The faint smell of wood and mustiness intermixes with the rich leather of All Saints shoes and accessories, creating an environment that is reminiscent of industrial factories at the turn of the twentieth century.

15 CONTEMPORARY VINTAGE

Raw materials and vintage fixtures and displays create an enticing environment for consumers to shop in while reiterating the brand image.

15

Case study: All Saints

Customer service initiatives

All Saints has mastered the art of customer service, allowing patrons to happily photograph store interiors while providing them with any information about the product or company they desire to know. While most retailers try to maintain a level of secrecy in their store design and visual displays, All Saints seems pretty transparent, allowing its customers and admirers to act as walking, talking advertisements for their brand. Just as the employees are customer-focused, so are their stores, which utilize technology (Apple iPads) to provide shoppers with an easy outlet for searching for out of stock or back stocked product that they are unable to purchase at the store. A system that works in conjunction with an already user-friendly website allows customers to quickly search for size, color, and availability, as well as have it shipped directly to them.

16 A PREMIUM MARKET RETAILER

All Saints is a niche market retailer, positioning itself between midmarket fast fashion and high-end retailers, offering a selection of goods that are well-tailored and priced.

"We are not a clothing company, we are not a retailer, we are more than just the high street. To take this to a global scale, you have to emulate outside the industry, and that is the distinction."

William Kim, chief executive, All Saints

16

Chapter 4 summary

At the store level, a retailer acts as the liaison between corporate offices and the consumer. While many believe this to be an easy task, it takes a lot of work to ensure the systems put into place can work for everyone involved, allowing for each stakeholder to have a positive, fulfilling experience. Stores have a great responsibility, overseeing many logistics systems that allow their brick and mortar plants to run seamlessly. From hiring and training associates to implementing loss prevention methods to ensure positive comparative increases at the end of the year, a store is only as financially successful as its management team is seasoned. These individuals work daily to facilitate those tasks within the systems that enable both their sales staff and store sales to grow.

Questions and discussion points

1. What are some of the key reasons a store manager might narrow down job responsibility to various assistant management positions?
2. Explain the difference between the back of house functions and front of house functions.
3. What are some of the benefits of conducting group interviews for a retail store sales position?
4. Why do you think employee training and development is crucial to a store team's success.
5. How do you think a store suffers internally from employee theft? How about externally?
6. How can poor logistic systems between suppliers and corporate offices affect a brick and mortar plant?

Exercises

Choose a retailer that offers both fashion apparel and accessories. Pay a visit to one of its brick and mortar locations and conduct the tasks outlined below, answering the following questions:

1. Walk around the store and take note of what type of inventory control measures the store currently utilizes. What would you recommend as an additional measure for a loss prevention tactic within this store and how would it help?

2. Ask a manager whether you can speak to her or him regarding her or his store's training system for new hires and seasoned associates. Try to gather information regarding training methods and the successes/ opportunities for the methods that they are currently utilizing. Reflect upon this information and provide additional ways for which the store management team can either continue to grow its current model or improve upon it. Be specific.

3. Utilizing the Internet, find a company that facilitates retail logistics. Once you have identified this company, choose one of the three ways discussed in this chapter that a retailer can grow through the utilization of logistics and identify whether your chosen retailer is currently using any of these processes. If it is not, do you think it could benefit from the implementation of your chosen process? Explain your answer.

5

STORE MERCHANDISING

One of the greatest enticements a retail brand can provide to its consumers is a visual aesthetic, created by a combination of analytical and creative tactics, that showcases the retailer's goods each season. This is done through the use of merchandising strategies, which connect carefully placed product to visual displays, incorporating brand attributes, shoppability, and circulation systems. Many of the merchandising tactics implemented in stores are retailer specific, but others are industry norms— suggested by consumer researchers and sociologists. In this chapter, we will look at the various front of house systems that keep retailers differentiated through form and function, providing consumers with an unforgettable shopping experience.

1 DRAWING IN CONSUMERS

Retailers need to draw customers in with strong brand representation. Department stores such as Liberty, located in London's West End, achieve this by creating large-scale displays that can be seen on multiple levels.

Merchandising and the front of house

Fashion merchandising is the scope of work within the retail industry that combines design, manufacturing, management, and retailing strategies, with the aim of providing consumers with a good or service, while also generating a profit for the company. This entails having the ability to understand business, as well as fashion, trends.

Various processes must be carried out to deliver a product or service to the consumer—all of which are completed by the various people working under the umbrella of the merchandising discipline. Buyers, merchandisers, planners, allocators, and visual merchandisers are some of the more common job titles that work to purchase finished goods, as well as to price, deliver, and properly display them in brick and mortar stores and online. Each corporate role delivers its part to ensure store teams have the most up-to-date product (and product knowledge) as needed for its store location and demographic, while taking into account current market trends. Store teams then translate and execute corporate direction, working to create a consistent front of house across multiple store locations—marrying style, trends, and business analytics to create a conducive shopping environment for consumers.

A CLOSER LOOK AT CORPORATE MERCHANDISING ROLES

Corporate merchandisers wear many hats and work with various other roles to ensure the right product is part of each seasonal merchandise mix for both brick and mortar plants and e-commerce. The larger a retailer gets, the more necessary it becomes for it to narrow the scope of work within its merchandising division:

× **Buyers:** work with merchandising and design teams to ensure there is a cohesive merchandise mix through material and product sourcing and development.
× **Planners:** analyze inventory productivity within stores, formulating promotion and markdown strategies as well as exit strategies for dead stock.
× **Allocators:** maintain proper inventory levels within stores and look to increase sell-through of product based on sales and merchandising trends.

"The market is like a language—and you have to be able to understand what it's saying."

Jil Sander, fashion designer

MERCHANDISING DIVISION

MERCHANDISING/ BUYING

creates seasonal collection

material/product sourcing

oversees total units/ stock levels

defines product margins

PLANNING

defines individual store mix

creates unit depth per store

oversee pricing architecture— promo/markdowns

RETAIL STORES

ALLOCATING

oversees delivery of inventory

maintains stock turnaround and sale density in stores

initiates store-to-store transfers

VISUAL MERCHANDISING

brand positioning and representation

oversees display and visual standards

promotions through display

2 UNDERSTANDING THE MERCHANDISING DIVISION

Each department within the merchandising division has a vital role in getting goods to stores and presenting them in a way that resonates with consumers. This ranges from the actual merchandise mix, to pricing, packaging, delivery, and eventually the visual representation of goods on the shop floor.

Merchandising and the front of house

The front of house is where all of the excitement in retail takes place, from entering the shop to meandering through the sales floor, which includes windows, shop zones, cashwraps (cash desks), and fitting rooms. This is where store teams are at their best, working alongside one another to provide a shopping experience that is visually exciting and consumer-centric.

Various areas within the front of house are hot spots for consumer traffic (and theft!), and this is where many store associates are often "zoned," or stationed to work. These areas are typically heavily stocked with merchandise, have strong visual display focuses, and act as key transition points on the sales floor.

Shop zones

When stores "zone" their associates, they put them into key areas of the store that facilitate the most foot traffic, deter theft, or aid customers in their shopping experience. Typically, retailers will zone their associates based on the key areas within the store (designated by corporate merchandising teams) that differentiate product through placement based on color, silhouette, fabrication, etc. Associates may also be zoned based on store need, which is facilitated by store management teams. Various zones often seen in brick and mortar stores are:

×   Entry zone: the store's entry point and where consumers are first introduced to the store environment. An associate placed in this zone is often deemed the "greeter," welcoming customers who enter the store.
×   Zone transitions: those areas on the shop floor that introduce a new concept, display, or product. Retailers with larger square footages will often have two to three zone transitions, usually denoted by visible changes in product, silhouette, color, etc. For example, a transition may occur from full-priced goods to a sale section or from the denim zone to the shoe/accessory zone.
×   Fitting rooms: areas designated for consumers to try on merchandise. These areas are usually situated at the rear of the store, near back of house entrances and/or adjacent to shoe lounges for consumers to sit while waiting for friends and family to exit the fitting rooms.
×   Point of purchase: the cashwrap (cash desk) areas, where consumers will find last minute, grab-and-go goods for purchasing, promotions, and/or fixtures that help to form a line to the cashier. Associates tending to the cashwrap (cash desk) are usually stationed to maintain this zone.

Again, each retailer will designate these zones based on information obtained from the corporate office and/or to meet the needs of the store. Usually, associates zoned in a particular area are required to service customers while maintaining stock levels and store visual merchandising standards.

3-4 MAINTAINING YOUR ZONE

Management teams will make daily break schedules, zoning associates based on availability and the ability to complete various tasks. An associate who has an interest in visual merchandising may be zoned to an area where displays need refreshing or updating. This allows the associate to service customers in the prescribed area while executing various visual directives.

Merchandising vs. visual merchandising

When it comes to retail stores and their front of house initiatives, it is important to be able to differentiate between merchandising and visual merchandising—specifically, the role of the merchandiser vs. the visual merchandiser. While both carry many parallel job responsibilities, each has a specific task that is vital to the success of the retail store.

More often than not, the words *merchandiser* and *visual merchandiser* are used interchangeably, with the assumption that the term *merchandiser* is simply a shortened version of visual merchandiser. However, the roles differ greatly and need to be identified so as not to confuse potential candidates applying for these positions.

Merchandising

As discussed earlier in this chapter, merchandising combines buying, manufacturing, management, and retailing strategies to help deliver goods to consumers. To do this, merchandisers need to have a strong sense for trends coupled with a high degree of business training. There are several job responsibilities that merchandisers are held accountable for:

× Communicate how the retail business will grow through line and brand extension.
× Ensure optimal alignment of seasonal sales goals within their departments.
× Along with the buying/design teams, develop brand assortments.
× Work with allocators and planners to ensure store product needs are met.
× Create product pricing strategies for each season.
× Coordinate with the creative team to ensure the proper execution of visual components to help drive sales.

As noted, a merchandiser's main responsibility is the financial analysis of seasonal buys—ensuring the products create the greatest potential for profit. To do this, merchandisers will coordinate with visual teams to strategically place product in stores through the visual arrangement of goods and displays.

5

A merchandiser's main responsibility is the financial analysis of seasonal buys—ensuring the products create the greatest potential for profit.

6

5-7 FROM HOME OFFICE TO SHOP FLOOR

Corporate merchandising teams work together to deliver seasonal goods to stores, looking at overall product assortment, fashion (and buying) trends, and consumer need. Once they have solidified each store's assortment, goods are sent with direction from corporate visual teams as to the proper execution of product placement, marketing, and displays for seasonal buys.

7

Merchandising vs. visual merchandising

Visual merchandising

Visual merchandising is the placement and arrangement of goods in a strategic and visual manner that conveys the brand image, enticing consumers to purchase through the use of sensory stimulating marketing. The art of visual merchandising can enhance the established merchandise mix visually; the lack of it can deter customers from gaining interest in the product or brand, sending them to competitors who invest heavily in developing and executing visual strategies.

Visual merchandising for retailers can make or break their seasonal sales goals, and all team members should invest in its execution and maintenance. Department teams should continually act on the direction of the store/visual manager and the home office to ensure brand consistency.

Prior to the product hitting stores, home office visual merchandisers will work with the merchandising/buying teams to obtain line sheets for the next season's product mix. Weeks of planning and presenting inspirational ideas to corporate teams begins the process of narrowing down a specific concept for floor sets, which will be developed at a mock store location or at a designated store within the field.

Before this happens, merchandisers will communicate to visual teams the various product assortments that need specific (often prime) real estate on shop floors based on the following criteria:

× The potential for higher profit margins.
× Large seasonal investments.
× Changes in trends or consumer demand.
× Introduction of a brand or style.
× Seasonal promotions.
× To move dead stock.

Determining where product will be housed on the sales floor is a crucial decision and is best decided by home office and store teams collaborating together to ensure product placement targets store-specific audiences.

"Visual merchandising (VM) is an indispensable retail discipline, consisting of a series of practical selling tools that are used to influence what and how much consumers buy."
Karl McKeever, founder and brand director of Visual Thinking

VISUAL MERCHANDISING KEY PERFORMANCE INDICATOR MATRIX

store architecture
space planning
consumer circulation
furniture, fixtures, and equipment

trading area
consumer demographics
target audiences
market segmentation

SITE

VISUAL MERCHANDISING

DEMOGRAPHICS

ENTERPRISE

BRAND

customer service
visual display presentations
business analysis
product assortment

brand representation
sales promotions
marketing/advertising
brand management

8 DEFINING THE ROLE

Visual merchandising looks at various areas as key performance indicators that can be analyzed through quantitative and qualitative methods. Uniquely identifying each segment's successes and opportunities will allow stores to meet or exceed projected sales goals.

8

Merchandising the store environment

Stores work hard to create a cohesive brand identity that resonates with consumers and keeps them returning each season. Store management will enlist entire store teams to aid in the process of transitioning from one season's floor set to the next, working hard (and often long hours) to achieve the company's directed visual plan.

Under the supervision of the visual manager, all team members will be trained on the company's visual standards and product assortment for the season, as well as the key product knowledge that needs to be conveyed to consumers. Even after seasonal floor sets, store teams continue to build upon the new aesthetic, working each day to maintain inventory levels and refresh displays—keeping the store clean and inviting for existing and new customers.

The store merchandiser's role

The store merchandiser and/or visual merchandiser adheres to a fairly strict daily routine, deviating only to react to business needs when necessary. From first entering the store for the day, to leaving when their shift is complete, these visual experts have one eye on the sales floor and the other on store-generated sales reports, using both to create an environment that is customer accessible and visually represents the overall brand identity.

9-10 ATTENTION TO DETAIL
   FROM FRONT TO BACK

   Visual managers need to ensure brand consistency is happening throughout the shop floor and within the store's windows. Attention to detail (ATD) is a vital skill to create the perfect environment for consumers to shop.

Having a strong visual eye and keen business sense, the person in charge of this department must be able to create innovative product displays and convey to the store manager and corporate offices how his displays and product arrangements have made a positive impact on the store's business. Typically, if the display or product placement is not generating the intended sales goals, the merchandiser will revisit displays and product placement in an effort to regain some of the lost opportunity.

Aside from arranging product and creating visual displays, the store merchandiser is also responsible for:

× Managing seasonal floor changes.
× Ensuring company image/culture is consistently represented at the store level.
× Translating corporate visual direction to the store through appropriate displays and product placement.
× Training and developing store employees on company visual standards.
× Utilizing corporate sales reports to analyze the store's business needs.
× Overseeing store marketing and advertising initiatives for the company and its brands.
× Protecting inventory loss through product placement, visual displays, and stockroom audits.

Store visual teams have a lot to accomplish in what always seems to be too short a day, so excellent time management and follow-up are crucial skills for this role.

10

Merchandising the store environment

Visual areas

Stores typically have devoted areas where the visual team can store furniture, fixtures, equipment, marketing material, etc. These areas must be kept clean and organized so that store assets are not damaged. Mannequins are a costly investment for stores, and mishandling or improper storage may render them unusable and replacements are usually not an option. Marketing materials are costly to print and should be handled and stored in areas where they won't warp or tear due to humidity or improper handling.

Organized visual rooms are a necessity for the entire store, especially during transitional floor changes and when the visual manager is not available to direct the staff when these items are needed. Keeping the marketing material safely held, mannequins neatly stacked or packaged (when not in use), and props stored correctly will ensure longevity and usability each season.

11 FIXTURES AND PROPS

Retailers spend a lot of time planning visual displays and even more in capital to produce them. Keeping these items correctly stored when not in use keeps them clean and undamaged for future use. It is a sad sight to see a retailer using poorly handled props and is something customers can easily hone in on.

THE DAILY GRIND

Below is the daily routine used by most fast-fashion visual managers, based on an 8-hour working day:

6:00am–10:00am: Enter store. Review any correspondence from closing teams and home office. Walk sales floor addressing depleted inventory levels and visual issues, looking specifically at windows, tabletops, and top-shelf displays. Walk stockrooms to access product overstock or replenishment needs. Participate in morning sales staff meeting and help management teams ready the store for opening.

10:00am–2:00pm: Continue to facilitate noninvasive visual changes on the sales floor, addressing department-specific needs and corporate direction. Make directives for new inventory placement, reviewing sales reports to ensure floor moves to generate revenue. Work with sales associates on visual standards training if necessary.

2:00pm–3:00pm: Walk sales floor to address any immediate visual concerns, especially in the windows. Step off sales floor to engage in necessary correspondence for closing teams as well as corporate offices. Create a to-do list for any tasks not completed.

Merchandising the store environment

Consumer circulation

The way consumers meander through the shop floor is referred to as consumer circulation (or circulation pattern) and is one of the most important factors to consider when fixturing the sales floor each season. Customers are drawn to specific shop floor areas due to product, visuals, or service needs, and a sales floor that impedes traffic flow (just like a busy street) will cause customers to give up trying to shop for goods, leaving them frustrated and dissatisfied, with no desire to return to the store. It is best for visual teams to evaluate their store's specific traffic flow each season, ensuring that the pathways are direct and accessible for all shoppers.

Areas such as cashwraps (cash desks), fitting rooms, and zone transitions often have the most foot traffic and need to have a greater amount of fixed space for consumers to navigate through. Leaving ample room for customers to browse is one of the retailing strategies that visual merchandisers employ, providing a greater chance of capturing the sale (think about shopping at your favorite store and how you prefer to have enough space to open a shirt up to see the extent of its pattern or to be able to put a pair of jeans against your body to check the length).

Visual teams that are aware of proxemics and the need for consumer space will be able to best fixture their sales floor based on the consumer demographic (and culture) they are targeting.

Accessibility

Another concern for the visual team is accessibility. Shoppers who have to overextend themselves to retrieve their goods typically give up and move to product that is within their reach. Often, retailers will put back stock items on the higher shelves and racks, but this does not stop consumers from trying to reach them. It can pose a hazard if product is too high (or in some cases, too low) for consumers to easily reach, so typically, shoppable product is stocked between two and six feet off the ground.

While there are various laws requiring retail shops to have a set amount of space between fixtures to allow easy navigation for disabled shoppers, many push the limits, fitting as many racks and fixtures on the floor as possible. It is a good rule of thumb to provide a minimum of 3.5 ft. (1.07 m) of space between fixtures, providing accessibility for those who have disabilities. Providing an accessible sales floor for all consumers will only better the shoppability of the product, thus providing increased sales and returning customers.

12 TYPICAL CIRCULATION PATHS

Three of the most common consumer circulation paths in retail are the straight, diagonal, and arbitrary plans. While each has its own pros and cons, it is up to the visual teams to determine which will work best for their consumers as well as the architecture/design of the store.

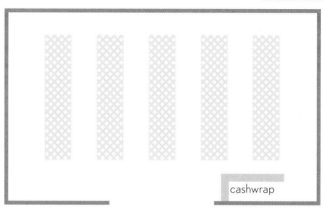

STRAIGHT PLAN

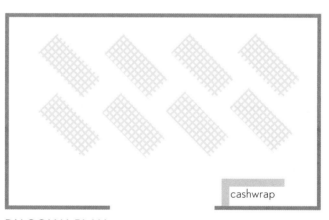

DIAGONAL PLAN

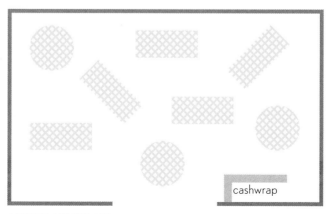

ARBITRARY PLAN

12

Merchandising the store environment

Floor sets

The biggest responsibility for a visual manager is to facilitate the seasonal floor changes that occur within the store. Planograms, or seasonal visual guides, provided by home offices, give store teams a detailed visual for what the ideal store layout for the season should look like, not taking into account budgetary constraints. It is then up to the store teams to translate the corporate directive into a floor plan and wall schematics based on the fixtures, product, and display elements that they have available in their store and within their budget.

Upon receiving the planogram, the visual manager will begin reviewing and interpreting the content, taking note of product or display props not scheduled to be received in her specific store. Working with the home office merchandising teams, the visual manager will typically receive a breakdown of product and delivery dates scheduled for his store, allowing him to effectively plan the execution of the floor move.

Starting with the windows, the visual team will typically work from the front of the store to the back, moving fixtures first and then products, incorporating the display attributes as they go along. This allows consumers to continue to shop with ease and accessibility, providing a non-intrusive environment as the store transitions from season to season.

When the floor set is completed, visual teams will photograph their work, archiving the accomplishment to reference for future floor sets. Often, the home office will ask for a layout of photos that show the process, completed floor change, and a synopsis of how the decisions made within the store have positively affected business.

13 SETTING THE SALES FLOOR

Visual merchandisers take into account what the store will look like during business hours and after hours when consumers glance in from the streets. Lighting is a key factor to ensure displays are well-lit and create impactful statements.

"If eyes are windows to the soul, then shop windows are just as revealing—they reveal the soul of the shop."

Debra Templar, founder of the Templar Group

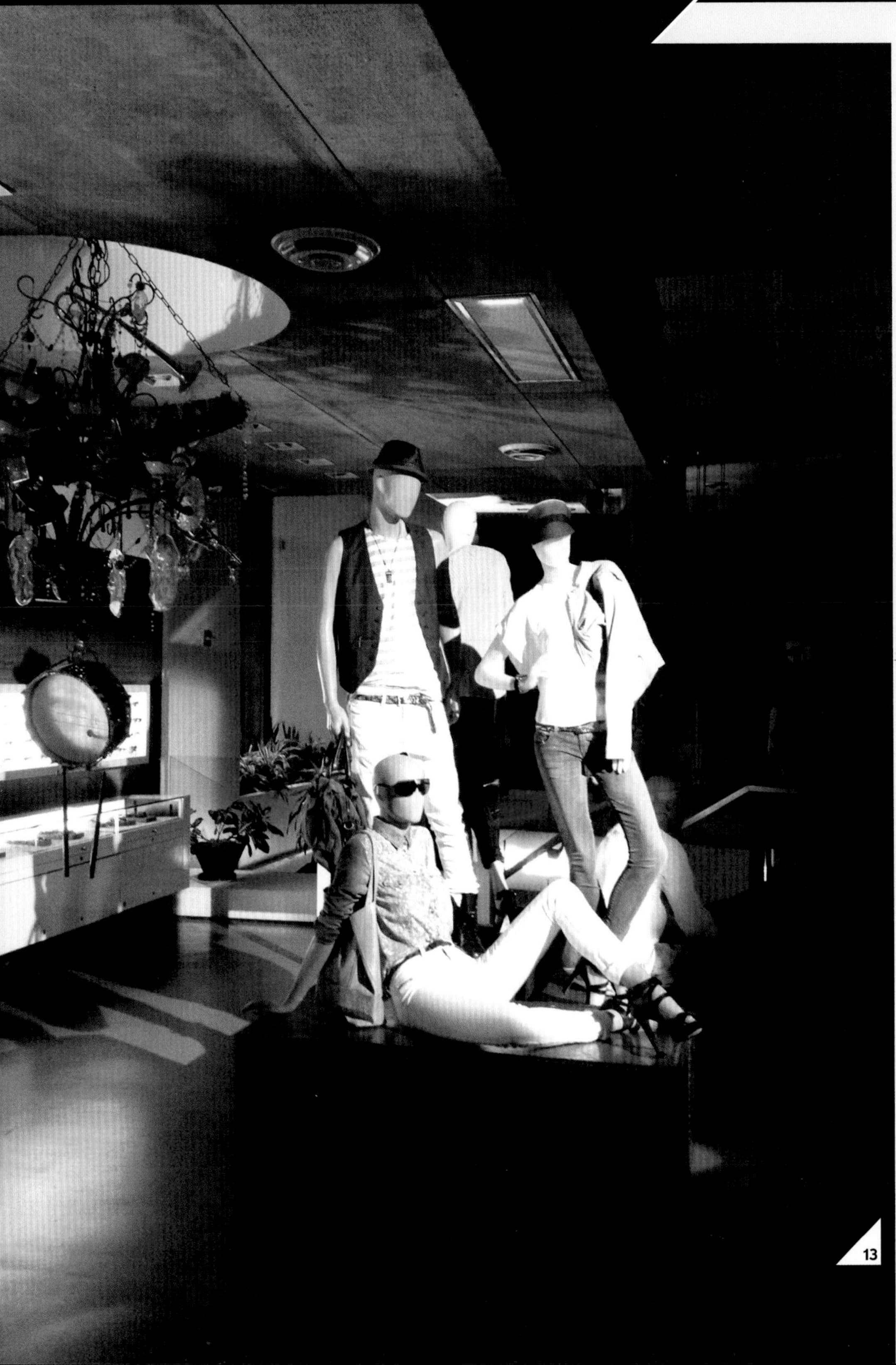

13

Interview: Alfonso Paradinas — Merchandiser

RÉSUMÉ HIGHLIGHTS

1990–1995

Attended the Universidad Autónoma de Madrid in Spain, studying business administration with a focus on international finance.

1997–2002

Worked in apparel wholesale sales for Hugo Boss, Spain, as the national sales manager for the brand.

2002–2004

Worked at Spanish footwear brand Camper, based in NYC, as key account manager for the US market. Moved to Custo Barcelona as national sales manager.

2004–2007

Launched Venga LLC to represent established European brands, such as Cool Hunting People, Sequoia, and Erva, within the US market.

2007–2012

Took a position at Polo Ralph Lauren as director of corporate merchandising for women's and men's footwear in NYC. Became director of merchandising for the menswear European division.

2012–Present

Founded D·Caged footwear, a men's and women's casual footwear brand, also working as a developing agent for US footwear designers.

14 FASHION FOR THE SOLE
D·Caged footwear has a casual elegance that makes them a perfect fit for the individual who keeps her apparel basic and accessories fashion-forward.

D·Caged

Home   Shop   About Us   DCaged2GiveBack   Collection ⌄   Contact

🛒 0 items

Interview: Alfonso Paradinas – Merchandiser

Q What are some of the differences in merchandising for footwear vs. apparel?

A Merchandising basics and the goal are the same, which is trying to build a market of relevant product that respects the philosophy of the company. One of the main differences is that when merchandising for apparel, you think of each category as a part of a whole brand look, as it will be presented together.

In footwear, you need to build the product that is in tune with the whole brand but also need to consider what your footwear competitors on the floor are doing, because most likely your product will get the highest volume on footwear-dedicated retail spaces as opposed to next to your apparel product.

Another difference relates to the construction of footwear, with its high costs on molds and lasts. This restriction makes the merchandiser plan a big portion of the line based on what needs to be amortized from a construction standpoint. Sometimes you want to give more space for designers to create, but it's not always realistic from a margin perspective. You then resort to working with different material combinations and slight changes to the constructions, adding freshness to the product and creating a different look, without incurring high costs.

Q How did your previous wholesale and national sales positions help you transition into the role as director of corporate merchandising for Polo Ralph Lauren?

A Merchandising for a big corporation requires a solid business background, and sales positions helped me get that sense of what the consumer and the market react to. As a merchandiser, you work closely with design trying to create a product that is true to the DNA of the brand but also a product that is going to be relevant in the market to deliver the sales numbers.

"Buyer–merchandiser relationships are essential to add relevancy to the product."

Q When you decided to launch D·Caged, did you feel the US or the European consumer market would be easier to enter?

A European markets are in general more avid for new brands, with a large number of multibrand boutiques that merchandise their own spaces to their taste and are always looking for newness. The US market, with dominating department stores, are slower in opening the doors to new brands, but on the other hand, when they partner with a new designer, the growth potential is much higher than in Europe. Both markets are great opportunities for any brand, but the approach is completely different.

Q What differences can you identify in the US market in respect to the European one, while you were a merchandiser?

A In the US market, the turnover is really high, and the product gets marked down much more quickly than in Europe. That makes for a less expensive product out the door and lower margins, but the volume is much higher.

When merchandising the collection, you build the line for Europe with more high-end luxury product. As there is less merchandise in the stores, the presentation of the product in Europe is cleaner, and the message of the brand is thus easier to transmit.

Q How do you envision the relationships between designers, buyers, and merchandisers to be at D·Caged?

A The stronger the link between designing–merchandising, the bigger potential for a solid business and brand integrity. Brands have to have a vision, but there is not only one road to achieve that vision. Buyer–merchandiser relationships are essential to add relevancy to the product. In my opinion, there needs to be a constant fluid discussion on branding between these three parties, reinterpreting the original vision to avoid getting stagnant.

Case study: Gap

One of the most iconic fast-fashion retailers today, Gap has been providing customers with the quintessential American heritage look for over forty years, offering fashion basics such as denim, T-shirts, and button-downs to families across the globe. As Gap continues to grow, it not only introduces the brand to new international markets but continues to instill its deep-rooted socially responsible campaign to those enlisted to help cultivate this growth.

There is something to be said for any retailer that can build a brand to the level that Gap has in under fifty years. Launched the summer of 1969 in San Francisco, California, husband and wife entrepreneurs Donald and Doris Fisher began their business partnership selling Levi's jeans and music. The Gap name was inspired by the "generation gap" of the sixties, and after claiming their stake in the retail market in a little under five years, they turned to private labeling, using their store name as the brand. The Gap was relaunched as the retailer for American fashion basics, offering a wide assortment of women's and men's apparel and accessories. Today, Gap has expanded to include not only apparel and accessories but also specialty market items, such as childrenswear and personal care products.

The reintroduction of the 1969 jean

Gap is most notably known for its American denim, rivaled
only by Levi's in assortment and style. Recently,
Gap saw a market need to offer premium, fashionable jeans
that did not compete with premium market prices.
To accomplish this, they relaunched the 1969 jean, branding
sections within existing Gap stores to house stock and
introduce consumers unaware of what made the company
so famous to begin with. An investment in a design studio in
Los Angeles, California, has enabled designers, musicians,
industry leaders, and most importantly, Gap fans to
collaborate on the curating of this product. A 1969 website
was added to quickly navigate consumers to this highly
in-demand product, and brick and mortar stores were
opened in Los Angeles, Chicago, and New York that
focused solely on the 1969 jean while incorporating
fashion-forward pieces from Gap's seasonal collections.

15 COLOR BLOCKING

Gap is famous for the color
blocked merchandising
technique, by which goods
on the sales floor are
organized by color.

*"Given how fragmented the apparel business is, coming to the
market with different brands and unique brands and multiple brands
into different channels and into different geographies is paying off."*
Glenn Murphy, chairman and chief executive officer of Gap Inc.

Case study: Gap

Socially responsible campaigns

One of the greatest contributions a retailer can provide the public is a socially responsible (and transparent) company that works with those in the supply chain to create a unified system for sustainable retailing practices. As one of the largest retailing firms, Gap acts as a leader for corporate social responsibility (CSR) initiatives, which many start-up retailers can strive to mirror as they begin to make their mark within the industry. Though some ripples have occurred within its system, Gap has moved forward with various internal programs that reach out to the community in an effort to help both, physically and financially, by working toward a stronger future for those involved.

As a global partner in the Red campaign—an organization to help fight the spread of HIV and AIDS in African communities—Gap has supported the cause by selling campaign-specific products in its stores and online. Co-branding with the franchise label (PRODUCT) RED, Gap has helped to raise millions for the cause by donating half of the profits from the sale of its products. Unfortunately, controversy began to rise when the media questioned how effective this co-branded campaign was and whether marketing initiatives were costing more than generated funds, but if anything, it helped to raise awareness of the epidemic.

"I look at running a store and running a business as playing a game, and what do you do when you want to play a game? You want to win."

Don Fisher, Gap Inc. co-founder

Since the start of the (PRODUCT) RED campaign and for years prior to this, Gap has worked to support communities in the US, as well as those in those countries where their suppliers are located. Most recently, they have launched the We Are Committed website (wearecommitted.com), which allows stakeholders greater insight to their CSR initiatives. The We Are Committed website is a blog for the company's CSR department, which employees over 70 people who are dedicated to addressing the various issues in the retail industry that can directly affect factories, nongovernmental agencies, and industry partners. Gap is a company that has been nationally recognized for its dedication to ethics and sustainability and will hopefully strive to be recognized internationally as it continues to grow its brand worldwide.

16 LINEAR FORMATION

Often using a variation of the straight plan, Gap creates niche areas for consumers to shop, making it easy to shop both floor fixtures and walls.

Chapter 5 summary

Store merchandising is a part of the retail industry that must seamlessly integrate both art and science in an attempt to capture the intended audience through strategic product placement and emotionally driven visual attributes. While merchandising as a whole is more concerned with product development, analytics, planning, and allocating, it is the visual component of the merchandising department that focuses on the visual representation of the brand through the use of display props, marketing imagery, and fixturing. Members of the store merchandising team work hard to provide consumers with an engaging visual environment that indulges their senses, enticing them to continue shopping season after season.

Questions and discussion points

1. Define the term *fashion merchandising*. What is the importance of integrating both fashion and business trends?
2. How do planning and allocating departments aid the corporate and store merchandising teams?
3. Explain the difference between merchandising and visual merchandising.
4. What are some of the visual responsibilities of a store merchandiser? What are some of the business responsibilities?
5. Do you think it is important for visual merchandisers to have strong business backgrounds? Explain your answer.
6. Why is consumer circulation so important for the store's success? How does a store merchandiser and/or visual merchandiser directly impact this?

Exercises

Choose two retailers, one in the midmarket fast-fashion range and another that offers high-end luxury goods. Visit both retailers and complete the exercises below while answering the following questions:

1. Walk both retailer's window systems and take note of display types, marketing, and product assortment. How are the two retailers' window displays similar? How do they differ?
2. Enter both stores and walk their sales floors. Take notes of any changes in key areas or zones and what visual merchandising attributes facilitate those changes. Do you notice any differences in the transition of zones between the two retailers? Specifically, how does the fast-fashion retailer merchandise its product vs. the luxury retailer?
3. After walking your chosen retailers' sales floors, sketch out how each store's fixture floor may look. Include the entrance/exit, cashwrap (cash desk), and fitting rooms. When finished, determine the type of circulation pattern associated with each retailer's fixture plan. Do you think this circulation plan is appropriate for the consumer demographic and price point? Why?

TRENDS IN RETAILING

6

So far, we have looked at various components of the retail industry that work together to create the well-oiled machines that we shop at—whether brick and mortar plants or online. These systems have been evolving since the start of the retail industry, at the turn of the nineteenth century, and have progressed in such ways that they continue to drive loyal consumers back to the brands they love. Retailers are becoming increasingly more aware (and proactive) of rapid changes in the marketplace and are turning to innovation in marketing, design, and technology, utilizing contemporary tactics, to help keep up with consumer demand. To complete our discussion on fashion retailing, we will look at the contemporary approaches being utilized within the retail industry today.

1 PUSHING BOUNDARIES

Contemporary retailers are pushing boundaries to attract new consumers while continuing to cultivate their current clientele. Fashion designer turned retailer, Joan Pastor, uses caricature mannequins in lieu of traditional realistic ones.

E-commerce and the online shopper

In today's competitive market, it is necessary for any brick and mortar retailer to have an online presence, providing multiple shopping environments for their consumers. In fact, because the Internet has become a market in its own right, many retailers are forgoing brick and mortar plants all together, cutting overhead costs until they are able to build their brand and consumer market.

E-commerce has rapidly become a forum for up-and-coming and established retailers to showcase their goods, allowing consumers to browse and purchase at their convenience. This shopping channel has become so popular, that many retailers have begun to separate e-commerce from brick and mortar plants in terms of profit source, looking at each as an individual business and therefore creating channel-specific retailing initiatives to help drive sales.

While this is good for forecasting a company's strategic growth, retailers must keep in mind that consumers do not view online and on-site purchases as being separate entities.

Many retailers are turning to outside agencies to gain insightful knowledge on what motivates consumers to shop online in an effort to help grow their businesses. A market research company, ForeSee, has linked Internet satisfaction on retailers' e-commerce sites to four things:

× Website functionality.
× Merchandise assortments.
× Price of goods.
× Website content.

Having a clear understanding of what is prompting consumers to return to your site will also provide insight as to how to capture new visitors who may be looking elsewhere for similar product and/or experiences.

"Consumers no longer see a distinction between online and offline shopping. Whether it's searching on a laptop, browsing main street shops, or hanging out at the mall–it's all shopping."

Sridhar Ramaswamy, senior vice president of ads and commerce, Google

E-COMMERCE FRONT END SYSTEM

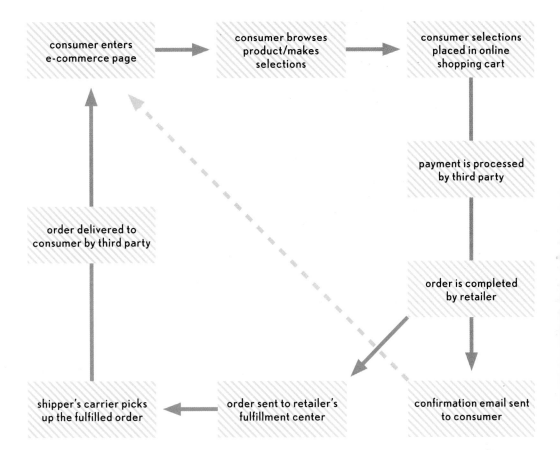

2 E-COMMERCE
   AT A GLANCE

The e-commerce process is
quite linear from inception
to delivery. Third parties are
typically utilized for fulfillment
of orders or shipping, but
sometimes other third parties
(usually between the consumer
and fulfillment centers) will be
involved. This is seen often in
international e-commerce sites.

E-commerce and the online shopper

Cross-channel integration

Consumer trends (and demand) are creating new standards within the e-commerce industry that retailers should be aware of. In a digital market, trends quickly turn to norms, and if a retailer is unable to offer what consumers expect as a standard service, they will quickly replace their favorite retailer with another who can.

A retailer practicing omni-channel retailing approaches needs to have a seamlessly integrated system that allows consumers to easily shop at brick and mortar locations, online, and via smartphones and tablets. Giving consumers the ability to walk into stores and purchase from their phones or browse online and purchase at a brick and mortar location will give the retailer a greater chance of sales conversions.

For those retailers that offer only e-tailing, having the ability to move between electronic devices with ease and little technical difficulty will also aid in conversion, while enticing consumers to continually visit the site via their favorite touchpoint.

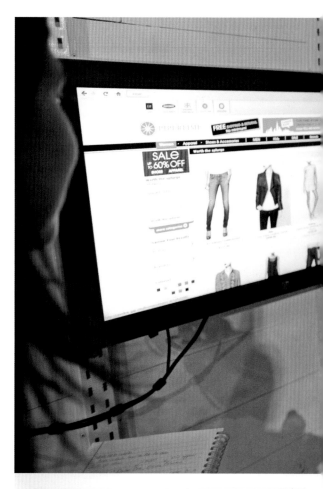

3 SHOPPING TOUCHPOINTS

How consumers purchase their goods varies, so retailers look to seamlessly integrate their systems on various touchpoints to make the conversion process faster and less complicated.

4

Shipping differentiation

Retailers have begun to offer consumers free shipping (and returns) via standard ground delivery. To do this, they build shipping rates into the price of the product, which aids in the conversion process because there are no added fees at the checkout page, putting consumers at ease due to not having to pay more.

Today, consumers want their purchases to arrive soon, so retailers are also offering additional flat fees to provide two-day, overnight, and same-day delivery services. The costs for these are significantly higher than for standard shipping and are often not sustainable due to the method of delivery (typically air carrier); however, some consumers won't hesitate to utilize this service if it means getting their favorite brand sooner rather than later.

Alternative currencies

As interest rates on credit cards continue to soar, consumers are looking for alternative payment methods for securing their purchases. Though still predominately used, merchant accounts (Visa, MasterCard, AMEX, etc.) are being replaced with payment processing sites, such as PayPal, Google Checkout, and Amazon Payments, charging the retailer, not the consumer, for the transaction fees often associated with using debit and charge (credit) cards.

4 FROM E-COMMERCE TO BRICK AND MORTAR

Piperlime, Gap Inc.'s online-only fashion boutique, is replicating its website in the real world with its first physical store recently opened in NYC. Jennifer Gosselin, senior vice president and general manager of Piperlime, demonstrates an interactive shopping experience and how Piperlime hopes to mimic the e-commerce experience in the brick and mortar plant.

Mobile retail, pop-up, and concept shops

Although brick and mortar plants have to some extent given way to e-commerce sites, retailers find that consumers still appreciate a physical space in which to browse, shop, and purchase goods. The question then becomes, how do retailers make the transition from an e-commerce shop to a physical space while encouraging consumers to openly embrace it?

There have been a number of ways in which retailers have introduced e-commerce stores to consumers in the way of physical spaces. Quickly becoming a marketing tool for retailers, mobile retailing, pop-up, and concept shops are an easy way for retailers to test markets, products, and brands prior to investing in brick and mortar plants or permanent physical spaces.

5-6 RETAIL POP-UP SHOPS

Quickly becoming a must have for up-and-coming brands, as well as those already established, pop-up shops are an easy way for retailers to test new markets or draw brand interest by offering short-lived samples or end-of-season sales.

5

Mobile retailing (the retail truck)

In metropolitan cities, the retail truck was a method traditionally used for the food industry, but fashion retailers have embraced the idea as a means to bring the brand to the consumer as opposed to the consumer to the brand. A converted truck that can accommodate a few individuals, allows customers inside to browse the brand, product, or marketing initiative. When the truck's time is up, it can easily pack up and be on its way. Many companies are testing markets with this system, blogging about its whereabouts to draw interest prior to its arrival.

6

"The old door-to-door salesman is too difficult in today's world, but we're seeing an uptick in bringing the product to the consumers."

Marshal Cohen, chief industry analyst at The NPD Group, Inc.

Mobile retail, pop-up, and concept shops

7

STORY: A CONCEPT SHOP THAT HAS RETAILERS WONDERING WHAT AND HOW

A 2,000-square-foot retail space in the Chelsea shopping district, NYC, STORY is a new concept that is making headlines due to its continually evolving gallery-like retail space. Every one to two months, STORY completely reinvents the interior theme, changing out fixtures, product, and design and creating a new message for retailers to tell and consumers to enjoy.

STORY is "a retail space that has the point of view of a magazine, changes like a gallery and sells things like a store," states its website, which also gives details about past, present, and future exhibitions. It is a fantastic space that offers a unique retail concept for consumers to engage in while providing an educational experience about the product and retailer.

7-8 A SHOP FOR EVERYONE

Pedestrians pass the BOXPARK pop-up retail mall in London, UK, where sixty shipping containers form a temporary retail mall. Concept shops like STORY are more permanent but still keep consumers interested by a continually evolving interior atmosphere.

Pop-ups

Pop-up retail shops have been around for years, previously being used for overstock goods and/or sample sales for high-end retailers and designers. Today, they are being used as a means for marketing, to generate buzz around last-minute location details and seasonal deals not otherwise seen in stores or online. While they have always been in the retail landscape of major cities, a large influx of pop-up shops are beginning to be seen in urban areas, as retailers and designers alike work to get their names out to new consumers in untapped markets.

Concept shops

Concept stores are those shops that are redefining the retail atmosphere through innovation of concept or product. When the term *concept store* is used by already established retailers, it typically means a change in visual appearance of the store design for the next round of stores to be built or renovated. However, the term is becoming more synonymous with those retailers that are unknown and are pushing creative boundaries in concept, product, and customer experience.

8

Retailer and designer collaborations

Retailer–designer collaborations started in the 1980s when American fashion designer, Halston, introduced a fast-fashion line for JCPenney, and they have evolved today into an industry of designer–retailer collaborations that are introduced multiple times within a season. Consumers want variety, looking to their favorite brands to provide them with out-of-the-box product that will make them stand out among their peers. Knowing this, retailers have turned to outside sources, just as JCPenney once did, collaborating on the design of various goods that allows them to market a more exclusive product to brand loyalists of both retailer and designer.

Retailers have quickly learned that no matter how loyal a consumer is to a brand, there are other brands that they are as equally invested in. To keep consumers returning to stores each season, many fashion retailers have begun working with high-end (or up-and-coming) designers to create affordable silhouettes under the retailer's label. Hired designers work with retailers to create silhouettes that reflect their design aesthetic and point of view but are created specifically with the retailer's target audience in mind. We are seeing collaborations across all retail types and from fast-fashion to high-end stores.

10

It is important to keep in mind that the cost for licensing the designer's vision, coupled with production costs, is not typically how the retailer profits. Instead, it is the press that is created from the collaboration that draws existing and new consumers in to purchase the retailer's other brands (typically private label) and where the retailer sees a profit due to increased traffic and a higher number of units per transaction.

9-10 GLOBAL COLLABORATIONS

Not just on national soil, collaborations are partnerships created by designers and retailers around the world, offering every market with a contemporary retailing industry the chance to indulge in coveted designs from both parties' points of view.

"The reason why some designer-retailer collaborations fail while others succeed is based on how well they understand the consumer's view of the specific combination of the designer and retailer."

Greg Petro, CEO of First Insight and *Forbes* contributor

Retailer and designer collaborations

Retailer and academic collaborations

Continuing with the idea of collaborations, many retailers are starting to look to university students and the university itself to bring new perspective to the market and allowing students the opportunity (and forum) to showcase their design work. The greatest opportunities are that the retailer can provide funding to the students to pay for materials and supplies or to the university by means of scholarships, creating little if any out-of-pocket expenses to be placed on the student.

11

JUST WHAT IS "MASSTIGE" FASHION?

Derived from the words *mass* and *prestige*, the term *masstige* fashion is used to denote product that was developed with the mass market in mind. It is typically licensed by high-end brands and designers and represents a downward expansion in an existing brand.

Michael Silverstein and Neil Fiske, authors of *Trading Up,* state that masstige fashion is "premium but attainable" and can be determined by looking at two variables:

1. The artefact is typically considered a luxury or premium good.

2. The artefact has a price point that typically fills a void between midmarket and super-premium retailers.

An example of this type of retail market is the Marc Jacobs brand vs. his Marc by Marc Jacobs and Bookmarc brands, which have high symbolism due to name association but cheaper price points.

11-12 DESIGNING THE LAUNCH

Students at Central Saint Martins College of Art and Design, London, UK, were given the opportunity to work with US-based retailer J.Crew, providing them with a hands-on experience many college students don't often get prior to graduation.

On separate occasions, Urban Outfitters has regularly collaborated with both exhibition and fashion design students from the Pratt Institute, New York, to create holiday windows and a line of women's dresses, respectively. J.Crew also enlisted the help of the students at Central Saint Martins in London, UK, to create a pop-up shop for the retailer when brick and mortar stores were built for the first time in the UK.

Designers, universities, and students alike are using their creative abilities to assist retailers in providing niche markets and products to their consumers. As national retailers further expand overseas, they will more frequently turn to collaborations, hoping to keep consumers satisfied and eagerly wanting more.

"When I was in EDI (Exhibition Design Intensive at Pratt Institute), I was able to work on a real project which was so much more valuable than designing a conceptual one. We are a company that thrives on creativity, and to be able to give students an opportunity to do something real is the greatest experience you can have while in school."

Julia Koral, display design manager at Urban Outfitters

12

Technology in the retail sector

It is difficult to discuss any trending topics in retail without bringing up technology—and specifically how technology is allowing retailers to cater to consumer shopping needs. As the industry grows but its tangible extent shrinks, retailers anxiously look for those tech outlets that will differentiate them from their competitors.

It is not just about those technological products that are in development and continually wow consumers when discussed but also about the previously introduced technology, which continues to develop and become cheaper and more streamlined for retailers to use:

- × 3-D printing: allows consumers to customize their products based on their preferences while allowing retailers to save on prepurchases, marking up, and trying to sell. This is fairly new to the market and mostly used for the customizing of accessories and lifestyle goods.
- × RFID: Radio frequency identification works by transmitting a radio frequency from a chip in the label/tag and can prompt videos or music to play as you near the source. Previously, this has been used for quickly ringing up customers' purchases or doing inventory.
- × QR codes: a customizable graphic that, when scanned, prompts the scanning device (smartphone or tablet) to provide direct access to the retailer's website, online discounts, blogs, etc.
- × Video commerce: A recent addition to many websites, this gives retailers the ability to show their products in real time, providing consumers with the look and feel of the product as it is being modeled. Sites such as YouTube and Vimeo are used to host the video (a link on the retailer's site will get you there), though some retailers embed the video directly into their websites.

13

These are just a few examples of the technology being utilized, which frequently updates. While all of these are great selling features for the retailer, quality of product, price, and customer service are still the driving forces for consumer purchases.

13-14 USING TECHNOLOGY TO ENHANCE THE CUSTOMER EXPERIENCE

It is not hard to believe that retailers are actively searching for innovation in technology to provide their consumers with an easier (and faster) shopping experience. Virtual shopping and QR codes are ways for the retailer to really engage the customer and foster conversion.

Interview: International Playground — Wholesaler and retailer

JOHNNY PIZZOLATO: RÉSUMÉ HIGHLIGHTS

1997–2001

Moved to NYC to attend school at Hofstra University to study performance. Worked at Armani and Urban Outfitters before graduating. Pursued an acting and music career but kept circling back into fashion.

2003

Produced benefit runway show for the Lymphoma Research Foundation with Patricia Field and her collection with David Dalrymple. Moved to Los Angeles and became West Coast sales director for Carlos Campos's first line—Guido.

2004–2008

Moved back to NYC to work with Guido. Started The Johns band and toured the US, performing while working with Brooklyn Industries, Carlos Campos, and AESA Jewelry, eventually taking on the role as Carlos Campos's market director.

2009

Co-launched International Playground with Virginia Craddock.

VIRGINIA CRADDOCK: RÉSUMÉ HIGHLIGHTS

1999–2004

Graduated from The New School University in the Cultural Studies program and minored in digital media.

2004–2007

Joined forces with emerging contemporary label Gingerblu as production manager.

2007–2009

Worked at Elizabeth Gillett in overseas production and handled private label sales. Consulted for Carlos Campos. Launched label REVIVAL, a collection of dresses loosely inspired by her vintage favorites from the 1960s and 1970s.

2009

Co-launched International Playground with John Pizzolato.

Q How did International
Playground come to be?

A International Playground
was founded in 2009
as a conceptual new
mode of operation in
fashion. After working for
independent designers,
founders Johnny Pizzolato
and Virginia Craddock
devised a new formula
for emerging companies
to have both a retail and
wholesale presence with
obtainable means.

The formula was seeded
from our own experiences
working with small designers,
their frustrations, and the
general lack of support for
emerging talent. We wanted
to create an incubator for
less commercial designers
and a platform to present
these brands to buyers,
editors, and the general
public in an impactful way.

Q What prompted your
transition from wholesale
representatives to shop
owners?

A The shop, or pop-up shops,
that eventually became
the retail store began at the
same time as the showroom.
We have always coexisted
as a retail and wholesale
entity—this is part of the
support system we offer our
designers and a strategic
choice for International
Playground as a brand.
The showroom started off in
the same space as the shop,
but we quickly grew out of it.

*"The world seems to get smaller and smaller every season,
and we see a lot more crossover than we used to."*

Interview: International Playground – Wholesaler and retailer

Q What are some of the challenges you face when selecting seasonal buys and how do you overcome them?

A Achieving the right balance of emerging talent and names that our customers may recognize is a tough balance. We are drawn to a lot of obscure international lines, but anchoring those with names people may recognize helps our customers trust the store to invest and discover in.

We also have trouble narrowing our selection, as the market is swimming with amazing designers right now, but we have only so much room for new talent. We anticipate carrying something we pick up for multiple seasons and building the visibility of the brand.

Another challenge is communicating the intrinsic value of a brand to our customers–to show the story and background of the designer, the specialness of the fabrics, the value in where the garment is made and who is making it. When we are choosing our buys, we have to consider whether our retail customer will understand *why* we think the garment is special while understanding the value. The retail world is so filled with collaborations and partnerships of high and low, emerging and established, and big box retailers that are hitting independent trends that it can be confusing to navigate emerging, responsible fashion.

Q How do you source upcoming trends that influence the product you purchase for International Playground, the store?

A We have the opportunity to travel quite a bit for our wholesale business, so we see what's happening in different fashion sectors around the world that informs our retail buys. One of our favorite places to visit and a great source of inspiration is Copenhagen.

We also look for trends in other cultural and design arenas—music, architecture, food, nightlife, advertising, interiors, etc. We also look to designer collections for seasonal inspiration, as these really set the stage for key colors, fabrics, and silhouettes that will be important in the coming season.

Q What similarities and/or differences do you see between the US and European fashion markets?

A The world seems to get smaller and smaller every season, and we see a lot more crossover than we used to. The US market still seems more timid and conservative than the European market, and big sweeping trends tend to catch on later here. Sportswear and athleticism is the current influence for menswear for the past few seasons.

In the US, however, the men's fashion market has been dominated by a more heritage, utilitarian outdoor look, which most of the European designers have fully moved on from. European retailers tend to be more international and risk taking in general, whereas most US stores focus heavily on US designers.

15 **DYNAMIC DUO**
Virginia and Johnny's partnership is not all work and no play, which is evident in the company's culture, store environment, and unmistakable products.

15

Case study: ASOS

Quickly becoming an e-commerce phenomenon, ASOS has set a new standard in the fashion retailing industry, making it difficult for other e-tailers to compete. Offering a wide assortment of branded women's and men's apparel and accessories, ASOS also sells beautifully designed private label goods, which have been showing up in the candid shots of fashionistas at design shows across the globe. This young brand is proving to the industry that making it globally means thinking globally (and responsibly).

Launched in 2000, ASOS (an acronym for As Seen On Screen) started simply by offering well-designed branded apparel, accessories, and beauty products to the UK 18- to 34-year-old market through traditional e-tailing channels. Fast forward 13 years and ASOS has since introduced international sites in French, English, German, Italian, and Spanish, making it an international powerhouse with eight language-specific websites for consumers. To provide the manpower to these sites and ensure its customer service remains in line with its humble beginnings, ASOS has international offices in France, Germany, and the US, with corporate headquarters in Camden, North London.

"In just nine years, asos.com has gone from niche get-the-look website, to massive internet phenomenon."
Grazia, women's fashion magazine

16 NOT FOR AMATEUR PHOTOGRAPHERS

When you are an e-commerce-only retailer, it is imperative that your staff knows how to use the necessary equipment for getting the best possible still and video shots to the online consumer.

Reinventing the online wheel

ASOS has continued to push traditional e-tailing strategies by providing its consumers with an interactive site that engages the audience with beautifully curated products, saturated color, and retailing strategies that are e-commerce specific. For instance, ASOS can be credited as being the first e-tailer to utilize a multimedia catwalk feature on its site, allowing viewers to see how the product they are about to purchase looks in action. This feature has had such a positive reaction from consumers that many other retailers have begun to utilize this innovative tool for themselves.

Another groundbreaking retailing strategy is the introduction of the Marketplace, which allows the ASOS global community to buy, sell, and trade goods—encouraging a unified mentality for sustainable thinking in fashion and retailing. In the Marketplace, you can sell as an individual or as a boutique/brand, with each seller having its specific stipulations as outlined by ASOS. Regardless of who is doing the selling, the global Marketplace is a fantastic forum for upcoming designers and stylists to share with the community fashion inspiration, trends, and product.

16

Case study: ASOS

Global growth = social responsibility

As ASOS continues to grow, so does its corporate social responsibility, making it imperative that it keeps consumers, as well as suppliers, informed of its intent. This has allowed ASOS to solidly build its CSR framework, appropriately titled "Fashion with Integrity," whereby employees work toward sustainable practices in the workplace as well as within their communities. ASOS has put various measures in place for ensuring that all ASOS stakeholders are on the same page when it comes to its goals. Some of its more recognized initiatives are:

× Ethical trade practices.
× Energy efficiency.
× Working with nongovernmental organizations (NGOs).
× Positive body image.
× Sustainable fashion.

All of the above initiatives are just broader spectrums for the more detailed initiatives it advocates for and participates in, making it a strong role model for up-and-coming retailers.

17 SETTING THE BAR

From warehouse to website to streets, ASOS has secured itself a place in the market as a fashion-forward e-tailer whose customer service easily rivals any brick and mortar store.

FREE SHIPPING TO C

Fur-free retailing

One of ASOS's greatest initiatives is its fur-free retailing practice. ASOS has made it clear to stakeholders that the use of fur in fashion is not acceptable, predominately due to the inhumane way it is sourced. To ensure it has well-informed team members and suppliers, ASOS provides guidelines on animal safety and welfare, distributes information to and trains its employees on how to identify faux/natural fur, and adheres to strict quality control checks. Some of the guidelines provided to suppliers for which they are required to adhere to do business with ASOS are:

× No use of fur, exotic leather, skins, or any portion of an endangered animal in its products.
× Do not test products on animals.
× Only source leathers, animal furs, and feathers from suppliers with positive track records of animal welfare.

For the industry, this is a huge demand, which ASOS suppliers seem to easily adhere to, giving consumers (as well as employees and suppliers) peace of mind that they are buying into a company that not only cares about them but also the world, of which they are a part.

🇬🇧 $ USD ▼

Welcome to ASOS. Join | Sign In

Saved items | Bag $0.00 (0)

MEN ›
✕KOUT   **£9.95 – UNLIMITED NEXT DAY DELIVERY FOR 1 YR**
UK ONLY (EXC. NORTHERN IRELAND)

This is ASOS

YOUR ONE-STOP
FASHION DESTINATION

Shop the latest looks at the best prices from over 850 brilliant brands, including the loved-by-fashion-insiders ASOS own label.

VIEW	VIEW
WOMEN	**MEN**

"As we grow into a global brand we make a greater mark on the world. This brings greater responsibilities, but also the resources and influence to bring about change. I am very excited about the potential for thinking around corporate responsibility to lead to solutions so we can meet our goals for growth and financial performance in an ethical way in accordance with our values. We are part of a global community, so we have to work with people and organizations around the world for our collective benefit."

Nick Robertson, chief executive officer of ASOS, Plc.

₱0 COUNTRIES

Chapter 6 summary

Chapter 6 discussed the importance of several trending topics in the retail industry, from the e-commerce retailer to the marketing tactics and tech systems used to draw in new and existing customers. Retailers continually experiment with various approaches to capture their audiences and look within the industry to reinvent opportunistic systems or strive to become pioneers for new ones. Their challenge with each customer's visit to a store or click of a web page is how to keep that customer engaged, loyal, and, most importantly, purchasing. Competition is a hurdle that all retail types must deal with, but retailers that focus their attention on the consumer, as opposed to simply trying to make a profit, typically are successful and sustainable.

Questions and discussion points

1. Why do you think it is important for a retailer to have an online presence in today's market?
2. What is meant by the term *omni-channel retailing*? How could omni-channel retailing make a retailer more globally marketable?
3. Which of the following do you think would be a successful research tool to use for an e-commerce retailer looking to transition into a brick and mortar store—mobile retail, pop-up, or concept store? Explain your answer.
4. Define the term *masstige fashion*. Provide examples of this market line not discussed in the text.
5. How are retailer collaborations successful for all parties involved (retailer, designer, and consumer)?
6. Do you think technology is a strong enough retailing tool to engage consumers? Explain your answer.

Exercises

Choose a retailer that currently operates on an e-commerce platform only. After thoroughly researching the brand and its consumer market, complete the following exercises:

1. Create a consumer demographic and target audience inspiration page, utilizing both text and imagery. There should be an equal balance of text and images that really show who your retailer's market is.

2. Next, choose a market you feel your retailer does not have a presence in. For example, maybe your retailer has little or no market in Vancouver, British Columbia (in Canada). Once decided, thoroughly investigate this market and create an inspiration page for it. Try to connect your trading area research with your consumer demographic by looking at key points such as age, interests, fashion preferences, etc.

3. Choose one of the methods discussed in chapter 6 for physically introducing an e-commerce brand to the consumer (i.e., mobile retail, pop-up, or concept shops). Creatively design your chosen method to reflect the information you found during your research and based on the e-commerce brand's identity. For example, if you choose to design a mobile retail unit, what would this unit look like inside and out? How would you design it so consumers could understand the brand?

4. Present your solution in the format you feel can best articulate your ideas (refined sketches, CAD work, digital media, etc.).

CONCLUSION

As we come full circle, ending our discussion on the diverse world of fashion retailing, it is difficult to forget how the ever-evolving retail industry has made significant strides since it began to emerge during the Industrial Revolution. Now with global presence in most metropolitan and rural communities, retail is engraved in our built environment and providing consumers with an outlet for their shopping behaviors while simultaneously inspiring them to seek out new shopping experiences.

We started by discussing various retail types and how they differentiate based on size, product, and consumer market. This discussion brought us to the introduction of multichannel retailing and the vast capacity that retailers have for captivating their audiences while continuing to grow their businesses. Brick and mortar plants, the Internet, and various other touchpoints have allowed retailers to reach their audiences faster, especially when social media are used as marketing tools. Various behavioral models helped us to better understand consumer markets and how a retailer builds its brand around them, setting them apart from competition and allowing them to move into niche markets, both nationally and internationally.

Corporate social responsibility showed us the importance of working with supply chains to improve systems that affect all stakeholders, especially the communities that support our retailers. Manufacturers, wholesalers, and retailers alike must work together to create a more sustainable and ethical industry that focuses on strategic long-term growth vs. short-term, profit-driven sales. Overall, retail corporate offices were the start of a more narrow conversation regarding the daily routine of brick and mortar stores, especially when discussed in relation to store management and merchandising, both working seamlessly to achieve a retailer's greater goals—conversion and profit.

Finally, we looked at those industry trends that are rapidly becoming norms. As retailers move from the traditional multichannel to an omni-channel approach, they meet shoppers' needs by making their experience as integrated as possible, allowing them to purchase when and how they choose. Various marketing strategies, coupled with technological advances, allow retailers to take their products to consumers faster, testing markets prior to investing in brick and mortar plants and transitioning into new trading areas. Retail is a lucrative business that constantly impresses consumers, engaging them with new retailing strategies that keep them hungry for the next big brand, product, and shopping experience—whether it be online or in stores.

Glossary

ATV
Average transaction value. This is the average spend of a customer, calculated by dividing the number of transactions by the amount of money received.

Back of house
A term given to those areas of the store not typically viewed by nonemployees and where job functions that require confidentiality occur (e.g. management office).

Base plate
Used to hold a mannequin upright. Generally made of glass or steel, they are circular or square in shape.

Bottom forms or trunks
Lower half of a mannequin, usually used for swimwear, lingerie, or underwear.

Brick and mortar
Used to denote the physical plant a retailer uses for conducting retailing activities.

Bust form/torso
A mannequin cut off at the waist, thighs, or neck. Tailored bust forms are produced in fabric, making it easier to dress and present product, thanks to the tactile nature.

Closed merchandising
Presentation of high-end or valuable products in locked cabinets.

Color blocking
Presentation of merchandise using color groups, sequences, and combinations according to color wheel theories and principles.

Conversion
A term used to describe a retail customer who goes from browsing goods to purchasing them. Also called sales conversion.

Core range
Products that are always in stock and that never change.

Customer journey
The experience a client has with a brand.

Design process
The journey and order of development from research through to design development and final piece.

Dual site/dual positioning
Merchandising products in more than one place. Especially relevant when a product can be sold with more than one item to enhance link sales and outfit building.

E-commerce
Electronic commerce is where the buying and selling of goods takes place on the Internet or via a system of computer networks.

E-tailing
The selling of retail goods via the Internet.

Fascia
External front of a store that surrounds the window spaces and usually contains the brand name and logo.

Floor plan
In architecture, a scaled drawing that provides a bird's-eye view of a specific area. In retail, floor plans are used to show fixture and display placement.

Floor set
When a retailer reconfigures the sales floor to accommodate a change in seasonal concept. This typically is scheduled seasons in advance and requires a lot of store manpower to complete.

Focal point
The point to which the eye is automatically drawn. Multiple focal points can exist in stores and windows.

Footfall
The amount of people walking through the store or an area of the store.

Front of house
A term given to those areas of the store that consumers have access to (e.g., sales floor, cashwrap (cash desk), fitting rooms, etc.).

Gross profit (margin)
The difference between the price of an item and its wholesale cost.

Hang tag
A tag attached to an individual piece of merchandise providing information about its composition, proper care, use, and origin.

Hot spot
Area in a store that every customer sees or passes by; has high footfall and exposure.

Impulse merchandising
Unplanned purchases. Retailers merchandise low-value items, such as socks, lip balm, and umbrellas, within the queuing area or next to higher-priced items.

JTS
Journey to sale (also known as point of sale; see POS). Consists of printed materials within the commercial environment, visuals, directional signage, promotional signage, and product descriptors, as well as advertising outside of the space, all of which support the customer's journey.

Limited editions
Designed to create urgency, ideal for increasing the average transaction value (ATV).

Link sales
Placement of one product next to another to create a spark or encourage the customer to buy more (for example, cleanser with an exfoliator, TV and DVD player).

Logical adjacencies
Similar to link sales, but the layout follows a logical sequence in the way a customer would use the product, for example, bras followed by underpants, shirts followed by ties, and so on.

Logo
Recognizable artwork to represent a distinct image or brand name.

Loss prevention
The set of practices a retailer employees to stop the loss of profit.

Markdowns
The reduction of or a percentage off of full-priced goods.

Glossary

Merchandising
The coordination, promotion, and sales analysis of goods within a retail establishment. One who acts on behalf of a store to complete these tasks is called a merchandiser.

Merchandising strategy
The plan for product positioning within the retail store space. It is based upon getting the right product in the right place at the right time.

MSRP (manufacturer's suggested retail price)
The price the manufacturer suggests to retailers that will provide a percentage of profit to the retailer while remaining positioned in a specific consumer market.

Omni-channel retailing
The idea of a more integrated and seamless customer experience through all available shopping channels—Internet, brick and mortar, tablets, etc.

On-hand
Inventory physically present in the store or at a company's distribution center.

Open merchandising
Fashion product that is laid out to be touched, picked up, and tried on by the customer.

Planogram
A schematic drawing of the retail store's fixtures, walls, and windows that illustrates product placement for the season.

Point of purchase
A retailer's designated area (or, for e-commerce, the web page) for consumers to purchase goods.

POS
Point of sale. Less accurate description for journey to sale; see JTS.

Price blocking
Merchandising products with the same price point together.

Promotion
A certain monetary amount or percentage off the original price of a good, for a limited amount of time.

Promotional lines
Limited editions, seasonal ranges or "buy it now" pieces that are merchandised differently to stand out from a brand's core range (but should also be consistent with a core range).

Pyramid format
Pyramid-shaped design format used in product presentation. This format is also used as a focal point central to an installation.

Research
Sources used to produce inspiration that leads to design development. Primary research is original content sourced by the researcher; secondary research is the analysis of images or ideas that come from existing sources.

Retail
A part of the supply chain whereby the sale of goods and services is provided to the end user for personal use.

Retail price
The highest price at which a retailer will sell an item.

Retailing
Those strategies employed by the retailer to help in the sale of goods and services to the end user.

Return

A transaction in which a customer gives back purchased goods in exchange for other goods or the original tender paid for the item.

RTV (return to vendor)

A term used in the buying office to denote those goods that have been selected to return to the vendor due to poor quality, slow sales, or any other issues deemed necessary for this action.

Rule of three or five

Merchandising theory based on the principle that items look better in groups of three or five (as opposed to even numbers). Mannequins are sometimes presented in this arrangement.

Sales forecast

The estimated sales a retailer expects to make in a given period.

Schematic design

Design that is conceptual and in the early developmental phases; rough sketches.

Seasonal merchandising

Merchandising that reflects the time of year, such as Christmas, Easter, Valentine's Day, and so on.

Sensory store environment

Designing an environment to appeal to customers' senses.

Shopping flow

The direction customers take on entering a store. The flow can be manipulated by walkways and circulation paths or by product placement.

Shrinkage (shrink)

The actual loss a retailer incurs due to theft (both internal and external) and paperwork discrepancies.

SKU (stock keeping unit)

The unique identifier for each product a retailer has in its inventory, which is used to check quantity levels during inventory analysis at the end of the tax year.

Spigot

Metal rod inserted into the leg or foot of a mannequin to connect it to the base plate.

Tailored bust forms

Traditional cloth-covered tailor's mannequins without heads. Usually featuring a central pole to adjust the height, these forms are easy to pin on to and tailor product.

Upselling

The effective use of selling skills and product knowledge to encourage customers to buy more; for example, the customer enters the store for a shirt and leaves with a shirt and matching tie.

Vendor

A person or company that provides items for purchase.

Visual merchandising

A term used to represent the promotion of goods sold by retailers through the use of display techniques, which includes product placement, fixturing, and environmental design (by means of visual design, art, and craft). One who acts to provide these services is called a visual merchandiser.

Visual merchandising

Putting the art and design into retail and commercial environments. Visual merchandising is used to communicate how to use or wear a product or service and enables the retailer to combine a range of components to entice the customer to purchase more.

Industry resources

Awwwards
Internet design creativity in fashion.
www.awwwards.com/50-fashion-websites.html

Coroflot
Coroflot.com creates better professional experiences for individuals in various design disciplines, all over the world. They are the largest and most active site specifically targeted for the hiring needs of companies that range from local operations to multinational industry leaders.
www.coroflot.com

EuroCommerce
An organization that advocates for fair, competitive, and sustainable retail and trade practices in Europe.
www.eurocommerce.be

European Association of Fashion Retailers
AEDT is a nonprofit association representing European retail enterprises specializing in fashion and footwear.
www.aedt.org

European Retail Round Table (ERRT)
The ERRT is a network of business leaders established to express the views of large retailers on a range of issues of common interest.
www.errt.org

FJobs
An international site promoting a plethora of fashion jobs around the world as well as industry-breaking news and information.
www.fashionjobs.com

National Retail Federation (NRF)
An association that advances the interests of the retail industry through advocacy, communications, and education.
www.nrf.com

Pantone
International color authority providing a standard in color language from design to manufacturing. Pantone also provides seasonal color forecasts to most industries.
www.pantone.com

Retail Design Blog
A blog by Artica that focuses on the behind the scenes of the retail industry. It was started to assist consumers, retail designers, and visual merchandisers by providing news and information about retail trends. Besides presenting interesting concepts, designers can comment on the blog and share views and ideas.
www.retaildesignblog.net

Retail Design Institute
An organization dedicated to the retail industry's creative professionals, including architects, graphic designers, lighting designers, interior designs, store planners, visual merchandisers, resource designers, brand strategists, educators, trade partners, editors and publishers, and students.
www.retaildesigninstitute.org

Retail Week

Retail Week is a UK-based online publication that delivers critical analysis of the retail industry's performance while providing a platform to celebrate the successes of the retail industry.
www.retail-week.com

Stylesight

Stylesight provides industry-leading content and technology solutions for professionals in the style, fashion, and design sectors. Stylesight offers global trends; past, present, and future information; and an online workspace designed to help industry professionals anticipate and analyze an ever-changing marketplace.
www.stylesight.com

Style Careers

StyleCareers.com is the largest, fashion-only job listing site on the Internet.
www.stylecareers.com

Supply Chain Council (SCC)

A global, nonprofit organization whose framework helps member organizations make improvements in supply chain performance.
www.supply-chain.org

The Fashion List

Providing an extensive online calendar for the international fashion and beauty community, The Fashion List offers subscribers current information on the sector's events and products, as well as industry-related newsworthy topics.
www.thefashionlist.com

Visual Merchandising/Store Design (VMSD)

A site geared more toward store design and visual merchandising, VMSD provides industry updates, introduces new technology, and presents various merchandising strategies.
www.vmsd.com

Women's Wear Daily (WWD)

Site of the US trade-focused *Women's Wear Daily* fashion magazine.
www.wwd.com

Worth Global Style Network (WGSN)

UK-based trend service delivering what is probably the widest available range of online fashion business-related services.
www.wgsn.com

Index

Index

Index

Index

Acknowledgments and picture credits

Many thanks to The Art Institute of New York City community, which has been incredibly supportive of my endeavors, working with me to help make my teaching journey successful—especially my students, who continue to inspire me each day. Colette and Nigel, sorry for driving you both crazy on a regular basis. Your support is more than appreciated. Having another completed project under your direction and encouragement is more than I could have asked for. To my family and friends who hate me for taking more time to pursue my career than to spend with them. You know I could not be where I am today without you. Thank you a million times over.

Picture credits:

Images used courtesy of:
Cover image: copyright Sybarite Architects (photographer: Donato Sardella)

Getty Images: 3, 7, 10, 14, 15, 20, 21, 32-35, 38, 41, 44 (×2), 45, 46, 49, 53 (×3), 64, 68 (×2), 69 (×2), 74, 76-77, 79, 80, 81, 92, 95, 98, 99, 104, 105, 107 (×3), 108, 109 (×2), 120, 124, 126, 127, 130, 131, 132, 142 (×2), 143, 144, 145, 148, 152-153 (×2), 157, 158, 160, 161, 162, 163, 168-169 (×4), 170, 171
Bridgeman: 12, 13
Kyle Muller: 29, 31
Tate Ragland: 55, 127
Jackie Mallon: 84-85
Dimitri Koumbis: 58-61, 86-89, 114-117, 125, 137, 154-156, 159
Shana Tabor, courtesy of In God We Trust NYC: 110-112
Alfonso Paradinas: 139
International Playground: 166-167